D1597188

THE PAINTED CAT

ELISABETH FOUCART-WALTER
PIERRE ROSENBERG

THE PAINTED CAT

The cat in Western painting from the
fifteenth to the twentieth century

First published in the United States of America in 1988 by
Rizzoli International Publications, Inc.
597 Fifth Avenue, New York, N.Y. 10017

Library of Congress Cataloging-in-Publication Data

Foucart-Walter, Élisabeth.
  The Painted Cat.

  Translation of: La chat et la palette.
  Bibliography: p.
  Includes index.
  1. Cats in art. 2. Painting, Modern. I. Rosenberg,
Pierre. II. Title.
ND1380.F6713 1988   758'.3   88-42741
ISBN 0-8478-0995-1

Originally published in France by Éditions Adam Biro under the title
Le Chat et la Palette.

Translated by Diane Guernsey
Typeset by Rainsford Type, Danbury, CT
Printed in Spain by Heraclio Fournier, Vitoria

FOREWORD

W hy this book? We love cats, and we love paintings. Why not put them together? The project seemed simple enough; bringing it to fruition, however, posed many problems.

We did not intend this to be a history of the cat: others have done that already. No more did we propose to outshine the poets and writers who have so admirably described their gracious, mysterious feline companions. Lady Aberconway's marvelous anthology of 1949, *A Dictionary of Cat Lovers*, relieved us of that task—everything, or nearly everything, has already been said. We wished only to select the most handsome cats in the history of painting. In order to accomplish this, we were forced to establish some guidelines.

They were:
— To include only Western paintings (thus there are no Egyptian, Chinese, or Japanese cats in this book, mindful as we are of their tremendous importance); and to include no drawings or engravings except in the introductory text.
— Not to use works by contemporary artists (so as to avoid the scratches of those who were not selected). Balthus was the exception that proves the rule. In contrast to our decision regarding the artists, we chose to reproduce only pictures of living cats. A curious point is that, to our knowledge, no painter has ever depicted a dead cat.
— In the color plates each painter is represented by only one cat (and not always the artist's best known; we realize the provocation inherent in our decision to replace Chardin's *Ray* with his *Launderess*).

In conception, then, this book is neither a lexicon of cat breeds, nor a history of the domestic cat, nor a dictionary of the cat in art. It presents chronologically some of the loveliest cats painted over the last five centuries. We hope that our readers will wonder—as we so often did—about the reasons behind the presence of the cats in the paintings we chose. Our investigations led us to include, at the beginning of the book, some generalizations on the iconography of the cat.

Every choice is arbitrary; it may also, sometimes, be mere ignorance. If we have willfully discarded several famous felines, we have not known of the existence of many other equally handsome but obscure cats. We hope our readers will help us to discover them. Painters have loved cats, but very often they have shown their respect for the discreet natures of their models by placing them in the obscurity of a chimney or alcove.

This promenade through the history of painting will reveal all sorts of cats—surprising, surprised, jumping, sleeping, uncanny or purring. The artists are no less diverse. We hope that this book, which has brought us so much pleasure, will also please those who dislike cats both alive and on canvas, and those who love them as well.

Théodore Gericault (?), White Cat, Copenhagen,
Ny Carlsberg Glyptothek.

THE ICONOGRAPHY OF THE CAT

THE CAT, THE DEVIL, AND ALMIGHTY GOD:
THE CAT IN RELIGIOUS PAINTING

Cats are familiar figures in religious painting, and those reproduced in this volume are only a small sampling of the many that have slipped, over the centuries, into even the most sacred scenes. One wonders about the reasons behind such success. The first question is whether or not cats are mentioned in the biblical texts or whether painters, in including them in religious scenes, have given their imagination free rein, drawing from popular tradition (oral or otherwise) that only later attained iconographic significance thanks to their work.[1]

Biblical Cats

Properly speaking, there are no cats at all in the Old Testament. The only allusion to them occurs in an apocryphal text—the Book of Baruch (6:21–22)—and is well known among cat historians, who mention it frequently, but seldom cite the exact passage. It occurs in Jeremiah's instructions to the Jews who were to be sent into captivity in Babylon. The prophet paints a dark picture of the Babylonians' religious practices and describes their gods as follows: "They are like one of the temple beams, gnawed away from within, so they say, by termites that creep out of the ground and eat them and their fine clothing, too.... Bats, swallows, and birds of every kind flutter about their bodies and heads, and cats prowl there as well. By these signs you will see for yourselves that they are not gods; do not fear them." Although this passage does not seem to have bestowed iconographic significance upon cats, it is noteworthy as an illustration of the role that the prophet reserves for cats: they are viewed solely as companions to the pagan gods. In Christian art, as we shall see, much of this hostile, negative perception of cats persisted.

In any case, many artists depict cats in biblical scenes, often quite important ones—as, for instance, that of Adam and Eve in Paradise before the Fall. The large cat that slumbers peacefully at the feet of humanity's first couple in Dürer's famous engraving of 1504 (see p. 8) has virtually been canonized, appearing with regularity, but with no scriptural precedent, especially in the works of Northern European artists. Among these are the paintings of Cornelis van Haarlem (see pp. 84–85) and—to name but two other important figures—Frans Pourbus the Elder (ca. 1540–1581), in whose painting in the Residenzgalerie in Salzburg (dated 1570 and resembling a Frans Floris) a cat is depicted awake; and Hendrik Goltzius (1558–1617) in whose composition, engraved by Jan Saenredam in 1597, a cat appears deeply asleep. The cat is not the only animal in any of these pictures; the painters populate their paradises with beasts of all descriptions in order to remind us that, according to the Scriptures, Adam was charged with naming all the animals (Genesis 2:19–21). In Dürer's garden of delights, the cat is, as it must be, perfectly peaceable: it has no quarrel with the dog and lets a little mouse scamper only a few inches from its nose. It is clear that it is Man's Fall that will shatter this lovely harmony among the animals. A second layer of meaning may be discerned in the purely narrative depiction of this idyllic world. As

Albrecht Dürer, Adam and Eve, engraving, 1504.

Erwin Panofsky has shown in his famous analysis of Dürer's composition, the cat personifies one of the four temperaments of man: namely, the choleric temperament. (In that case, the ox would represent the phlegmatic, the hare the sanguine, and the elk the melancholic temperaments, respectively.)[2] In the course of complex scholarly speculations, an almost secular traditional symbolism has attached itself to the sacred theme. It states that before Sin existed the four temperaments were perfectly balanced in Man, who is God's creation, and that this equilibrium was evidently disturbed by the Fall.

Another story in Genesis, that of Noah and the Flood, naturally furnished artists with the opportunity to depict cats; but the feline couples in these scenes (see Castiglione, p. 90) are on the same footing as the other animals. Even less significant or merely anecdotal are the cats that appear here and there, for no apparent reason, in diverse Old Testament scenes. A cat sits near a dog in *Abraham's Sacrifice* by Benozzo Gozzoli (ca. 1422–1497), one of the frescoes at Campo Santo in Pisa, done in about 1468–1484 and badly damaged in World War II; another cat licks its chops under a table in a work by the Flemish painter known as the Master of the Story of Joseph (late fifteenth to early sixteenth century), in which Joseph interprets the dreams of Pharaoh's baker and cupbearer (New York, Metropolitan Museum of Art). Still another cat sits comfortably at the hearthside in *Esau Selling His Birthright to Jacob* by Michel Corneille (see pp. 110–11), a scene also painted by Luca Giordano (1634–1705), who included a dog in it as well (Valladolid, Provincial Museum).

One could find many other cats that have furtively and silently insinuated themselves into the company of biblical figures by way of their privileged status as domestic pets. Likewise, in the majority of pictures inspired by the New Testament, artists have skillfully juggled the cat's two aspects—its role as an animal charged with complex symbolism, and as man's companion, which allows it to be introduced discreetly into the traditional compositions of sacred scenes.

Evangelical Cats

The Gospels mention some animals by name: birds and sheep figure in the most beautiful and poetic images in Christ's parables, and the dogs that licked poor Lazarus's ulcers helped confirm his status as the archetype of human misery. But cats are no more highly thought of in the New Testament than in the Old.

Nonetheless, the Gospels' essentially narrative character has tempted artists into many "realistic" departures from the original text. Thus cats have found their way into scenes from Christ's life, mainly of his childhood. These include the Annunciation and several episodes from his public life, such as the Wedding at Cana, the dinner with Simon, and especially the Supper at Emmaus, which took place after the Resurrection. This book contains no fewer than fifteen New Testament scenes containing cats. So common are these tableaux that many cat historians, aping one another, have claimed the existence of a "Christian legend" in which a female cat gave birth to a litter of kittens in the stable at Bethlehem at the same moment that Jesus was born.[3]

No more than that was needed for them to imagine that the cat is the same cat as in the Annunciation scenes—one already encounters it in paintings of the Virgin's mother Saint Anne—and that its descendents accompany Christ up to his Crucifixion and after his Resurrection. Thus this dynasty of New Testament cats forms a sort of feline counterpart to King David's line of descendants.

This train of thought seems to have originated in a book entitled *The Gospel of the Holy Twelve,* written by a certain Reverend G. J. Ouseley and published in London in 1923. This "new," fantastical Gospel was supposedly transcribed from a Christian document preserved at a Buddhist monastery in Tibet.[4] In addition to the episode involving the mother cat, according to this text, Christ had dealings with cats on at least two other occasions. First, he saved a cat from the torments of "a band of idlers of the lowest kind"; later, he fed and refreshed a young cat dying of hunger and thirst, in order to show that the Almighty had bestowed upon man and beast the same breath of life.[5] This pleasant Gospel is known only to cat fanatics and is, at best, of marginal importance.

The innumerable cats of all colors and kinds, waking and sleeping, that we see depicted near the Virgin or Judas are not there solely at the artist's whim, or merely to lend a touch of realism and intimacy to a sacred scene. The cat's significance is best exemplified in *The Supper at Emmaus* by Philippe de Champaigne (see pp. 108–109) and *The Infant Jesus Asleep* by Charles Le Brun (see pp. 112–13) in both of which cats are well to the fore. Champaigne, moreover, put a tiger-striped cat in his great *Meal with Simon the Pharisee,* which he painted for the Val de Grâce (Nantes, Musée des Beaux-Arts, depository of the Louvre). At his Royal Academy lecture in 1668 on Poussin's celebrated *Eliezer and Rebecca* (now at the Louvre), a lively debate took place about the camels (mentioned in the biblical texts) that the artist had seen fit to leave out.[6] Champaigne regretted their absence, in the interests of historical truth; but Le Brun responded that the painter is free to omit any "bizarre object" that would distract the viewer's eye from the principle subject. And, he later added, the ox and the ass (missing from the Gospels) are "pure chimeras," and completely unnecessary to a Nativity scene. Certainly, their exchange included not the least allusion to cats; but from Le Brun's firm stance on this issue we can deduce that, in bringing a cat so obviously into his *Holy Family,* he considered the animal neither inconvenient nor superfluous. As for Philippe de Champaigne, as he placed a cat openly in his *Supper at Emmaus,* it was surely with a precise intention in mind, so steeped in scholarly Christian iconography was the Port-Royal painter.

The scene into which painters most often put cats is doubtless the Annunciation.[7] Very early on, artists in every country put a cat not far from the Virgin—often as a mere spectator, as in the *Annunciation* of Jan de Beer (ca. 1475–ca. 1518)[8] or, much later, in the works of the Neapolitan artists Francesco de Mura (1692–1782), at the Santa Maria dell'Ainto, and Gaspare Traversi (1732–1769), at the Carthusian church of San Martino. Occasionally in these scenes, the cat seems to question the onlooker, as it does, staring insistently at us, in an Annunciation attributed to the painter Gian Francesco Bembo, active in Cremona during the first half of the sixteenth century (parish church of Isolo Dovarese). Moreover, as we see in a painting (ca. 1486–1487) at the church of Saint Bernard at Wroclaw, the cat completely ignores the holy event that is taking place: it concentrates, rather, on a little bird that has just time to fly away. It plays with a work basket that the Virgin has dropped, her task interrupted by the angel's arrival, in a painting by Pomponio Amalteo (1505–1558), executed ca. 1535 in the church of Santa Maria dei Battusti at San Vito al Tagliamento. The cat does this, that is, if it is not sleeping deeply (see Barocci, pp. 66–67) or zigzagging across the scene like a furious little black devil (see Lotto, pp. 58–59). Clearly, all of these cats are connected with an idea both ancient and very deeply fixed in our psyches (one will always

Giuseppe Mazzuoli, The Wedding at Cana, Private Collection.

find it more or less infused, even in secular iconography)—an idea that the cat is on the side of the forces of evil. The roots of the concept are certainly to be found in popular beliefs, which here intervene in the Christian narrative. We then understand that the artists had no need of Scriptural references in order to inscribe cats in the register of sacred history.

An excellent example of this is the motif often encountered in paintings of the Holy Family: a cat watching (or stalking) a goldfinch held either by the Infant Jesus (studio of Cosmé Tura, see p. 45) or by the young John the Baptist, as in Barocci's famous work (ca. 1574–1575; London, National Gallery). The symbolism is clear and a bit simplistic: the goldfinch, as its name suggests in French (*chardonneret*) and in Italian, Dutch and German (see Pencz, pp. 70–71), is particularly fond of thistles (*chardons*); hence, it is traditionally interpreted as an allusion to the crown of thorns and to Christ's Passion.[9] In threatening the bird, the cat menaces the Passion through which Christ will save humanity. The cat (Evil) opposes Salvation. There we have the manner—figurative, almost naive, and circuitous—in which a role is bestowed upon the cat in scenes of Christ's infancy.

There are also many Holy Families depicted with cats but without

Frans Floris, Holy Family, Musée du Louvre.

goldfinches. They are found particularly among works of the Italian school, in which the title *Madonna with Cat* is familiar and applies equally to a Leonardo sketch (London, British Museum) and to Giulio Romano's *Madonna of the Cat* (see pp. 62–63). The animal's pose in these pictures varies considerably: it may stare insolently out at the viewer (Romano) or sleep (see Vermeyen, pp. 80–81; Murillo, pp. 96–97; Le Brun, pp. 112–13; Rembrandt, pp. 100–101). The cat dozes in a *Holy Family* by Frans Floris (1519/1520–1570, p. 10) and his assistants (Paris, Musée du Louvre). The cat may give away its presence through some eccentricity: in a *Holy Family* by Jordaens (ca. 1615; Brussels, Musées royaux des Beaux-Arts), a cat snatches at a wicker-work cage and (a fleeting detail, very sharply observed) causes the water from the "mangers" to overflow. The Spanish painter Fernandez de Navarette (1526–1579) depicted a cat and a dog united in covetous longing for the same bone in the foreground of his *Holy Family*.

The Nativity, for its part, has given rise to what is certainly the most affecting of paintings in the eyes of cat lovers. Again, the artist is Barocci (see p. 11). A cat nurses its young, at the feet of the Virgin, who rocks the Infant Jesus. (The original picture, which was at the Uffizi in Florence, was almost completely burned at the end of the eighteenth century, and the composition exists only in engravings or copies.)[10] This maternal cat is probably the source of all the extravagant ideas discussed earlier. It is obvious that, for Barocci, iconographic purpose unites with a passion for felines. Perhaps the work's tenderness (the mother cat loves and cares for her young as the Virgin does) softens the malevolent significance cats are usually assigned.

When cats are depicted in Christ's public life, it is always at feasts or festivals where, as peripheral but noteworthy and easily spotted figures, they mingle with the other guests. At times, the cat will be almost as imposing as the vases in which the water changes to wine, as in *The Wedding at Cana* (Private Collection, p. 10) by Giuseppe Mazzuoli (1536–1589). Then again, it may devote itself to furiously clawing an earthenware jar that, in Veronese's picture, has been transformed into a sumptuous "Renaissance" object—as if the animal were impertinently mocking great art (see pp. 68–69). Another of Veronese's cats is at play under the table in the *Dinner with Levi* (Venice, Galleria dell'Accademia).

In his *Last Supper*, Tintoretto did not hesitate to include a cat standing on its hind legs and surveying a huge basket containing the used dishes (Venice, San Giorgio Maggiore, ca. 1592–1594). Still more significant is the cat next to Judas in Ghirlandaio's *Last Supper* (see pp. 46–47) and in that by Luini (1512–1532) at the refectory of Santa Maria degli Angeli in Lugano. In both, the traitorous apostle clutches his purse of coins, a cat crouched at his feet. Once more, the unfortunate beast is obliged to play Evil's companion—if not its accomplice.

Another motif of interest is that of a pitiless confrontation between a cat and dog,[11] often over a bone; this frequently occurs in scenes of the Last Supper, such as that of Cosimo Rosselli (see pp. 50–51). In the work by Simone de Magistris (ca. 1534–after 1600) the two animals are about to chase each other all around Judas's stool, a strategic spot, since we can see pinned to the seat a large sheet of paper with the painter's name and the date, 1598 (church of San Ginesio). This picturesque face-off occurs in other New Testament scenes: for example in one showing the Magdalen kneeling at Christ's feet, painted in 1523 by the Spanish artist known as the Maestro de Alcira (Valencia, Museo Catedralicio y Diocesano); or in *The Dance of Salome* (see p. 11), a fresco by Giovanni Battista Naldini (1537–1591) at the church of the Trinita dei Monti in Rome (here the cat is almost under the cruel dancer's feet).

Obviously, the confrontation is not merely between two traditional foes; it is above all a depiction of the combat of Good and Evil, the dog symbolizing devotion to one's master and thus setting a noble example for Christians, who must be faithful to God's commandments.

The last evangelical repast to which cats are invited is the Supper at Emmaus during which the Resurrected Christ revealed himself. We encounter cats in paintings of this scene by Pontormo (see pp. 60–61), Bassano (see pp. 64–65), Champaigne (see pp. 108–109), Veronese (Paris, Musée du Louvre) and Jordaens (Dublin, National Gallery);

Giovanni Battista Naldini, The Dance of Salome, Rome, Church of the Trinita dei Monti.

Holy Family, copy after Barocci, formerly at the Metropolitan Museum of Art, New York.

Théodore van Loon, The Visitation, Brabant (Belgium), Church of Montaigu.

the list is endless. After Christ's Crucifixion and Resurrection, what role will befall the cat? Bernard Dorival contributes a compelling speculation in connection with Philippe de Champaigne's *Supper at Emmaus*.[12]

The painter's library contained a work that was well-known at the time, the *Commentaires hiéroglyphiques* by Valeriano (first published in 1556 in Basel, in Latin, but translated into French and republished many times). Many of Champaigne's religious works bear incontestable marks of the influence of this compilation of often obscure or convoluted symbolic meanings. Thus, according to Valeriano, the cat is the hieroglyph of the moon, and through this of beginnings and endings (*ortus et obitus rerum*), and hence it signifies that the Resurrected Christ will never die, and that his sacrifice is eternal. For once, the cat is entrusted with a benign and optimistic symbolic meaning. But what shall we make of the cats in Suppers at Emmaus painted prior to the appearance of Valeriano's lexicon—those of Pontormo or Bassano (see pp. 60–61 and 64–65), for instance? We must remind ourselves that the authors of iconographic compendia invented nothing and contented themselves with documenting the ideas that were circulating at the time among artists and their patrons.[13]

The life of the Virgin also furnished opportunities to include cats. We see them in depictions of the Annunciation to Saint Anne by artists as far back as Ugolini di Prete Ilario (active in Orvieto from 1357 to 1380), who created the fresco in the chancel of the cathedral in Orvieto. A little later another Italian, Arcangelo di Cola da Camerino (active from 1416 to 1429), placed an ugly little cat—almost a rat—in his *Visitation* (Philadelphia, Philadelphia Museum of Art). The Flemish painter Théodore van Loon (1585–1660) did the same (this time, however, the animal was neatly rendered) in a Visitation, one of seven paintings dedicated to the life of the Virgin that he did between 1623 and 1628 for the Church of Montaigu in Brabant (see p. 12). Cats also appear in depictions of the Virgin's birth, principally Italian works such as those by Scarsellino (ca. 1551–1620; Modena, Galleria Estense) and Luca Giordano (Vienna, Kunsthistorisches Museum), but also in a painting by the Spaniard Fernando de Llanos (Cathedral of Valencia; 1507).

Saintly Cats

In a work dedicated in 1951 to cats, Marcel Uzé, one of their staunchest defenders, bitterly deplored the fact that they were not used as any saint's attribute, whereas, for example, a dog accompanies Saint Roch, a stag Saint Hubert, and a pig Saint Anthony. In protest of this flagrant injustice, he petitioned Pope Gregory I (a great cat lover, as the cats at the Vatican remember) in pressing terms: "Saint Gregory, pity the little cats, who did not commit the Original Sin and who did not eat birds in Paradise, where all Animals lived in peace."[14] But attempts at revision on the matter of saints have long been with us—from those of the Counter-Reformation Bollandists, who edited and published the lives of the saints in the *Acta Sanctorum*, to those of the scholarly and implacable church historian Monseigneur Louis-Marie-Olivier Duchesne at the turn of the century—and Marcel Uzé's petition was denied.

We can console ourselves somewhat with the thought that it is not entirely true that *no* cat is linked with a saint. To be sure, the cat's saint is not well known; he is a certain Cado or Cadoc of Gallic origin, who lived in sixth-century Brittany.[15] There, it is said, he tricked the Devil with the help of a cat. Satan had promised to build a bridge connecting the island of Batz to the mainland, on condition that the first creature to cross it would be his. Saint Cadoc induced a cat to cross. Thus, once more, the unfortunate beast is associated with the Devil—sacrificed this time, it is true, in a good cause. According to Louis Réau, the Bretons invoked Saint Cado in treating maladies of the eyes (as we shall discover, cats are associated with Sight in secular allegories, and this, perhaps, lies behind their popular veneration) and for ulcers (doubtless an allusion to the cruel scratches felines can inflict).

A popular engraving, published in Rennes in 1863, illustrates the legend (see p. 13). The saint and the Devil, gigantic figures, stand on the bridge, holding between them a poor little cat, very badly drawn. It is worth noting that Maurice Denis, a Breton in spirit and a great cat lover (see p. 201), owned several prints of this engraving. As a Nabi enamored of flat, decorative modernist tints, he owed it to himself to honor also the freshness of these naive images.[16]

The cat has occasionally been associated with Saint Yves. A Breton also (from Tréguier), Saint Yves is certainly better known than Cado, but his link with cats is both more tenuous and more arcane—it seems to have remained in the realm of hagiographic commentary. Yves was himself a lawyer and the patron saint of the profession; his cat is an allusion to the wounds inevitably suffered in the course of all due process.[17]

Saint Gertrude, the abbess of Nielles, is linked with cats only indirectly, from the viewpoint of their victims, rats and mice. Gertrude was invoked in controlling vermin, and in the fierce battle she must have waged she indeed had need of cats as her acolytes. She was invoked also in the treatment of feline illnesses, if we may believe a very erudite treatise on Christian iconography, written in the 1800s by Monseigneur Barbier de Montault.[18] Unhappily, rats and mice have supplanted cats in pictures of the Saint. Thus, on the wing of an altarpiece (Utrecht, Gemeentemuseum) painted by Jan Van Scorel (1495–1562) for the Lokhorst family in about 1526, Gertrude brandishes a parchment on which are shown several mice with the inscription *Super Latrones Vicit* (She Vanquishes Pilferers). But there is no cat there to help her. We must draw a connection between Saint Gertrude's battle and an Irish tradition (more legendary than hagiographic) according to which the mouse was created by Lucifer and the cat by Saint Michael: in both cases the cat sides with Good against Evil.[19]

Plenty of other cats appear in the company of eminent saints, but as incidental embellishments. Thus the shriveled cat near Saint Jerome in Antonello da Messina's picture (see pp. 48–49) does not distract us from the lions that are the customary companions of the Father of the Church (as, for example, in Dürer's engraving). By the same token, the cat in confrontation with a dog in the foreground of the fresco (1505–1508) by Sodoma (1477–1549), that depicts Saint Benoit feeding the sparrows at the cloister of Monte Oliveto Maggiore, has no part in the saint's iconography. This is true also of the cat (in the company of a dog) that prepares to eat in the foreground of *The Birth of John the Baptist* (Turin, Museo Civico), a colored print that critics generally agree is by Jan van Eyck (1390/1400–1441). Equally unrelated is the cat asleep in the corner of *The Birth of Saint Wenceslas* (Prague, National Gallery), painted ca. 1641 by the Prague artist Karel Skreta (1610–1674).

For the Spanish painter Vicente Carducho (1576–1638), the small cat that plays with a tortoise in the austere study of the fifteenth-century Carthusian Denis (La Coruna, Escola de bellas Artes) is

Saint Cado, engraving published in Rennes in 1863, Paris, Musée national des Arts et Traditions populaires.

13

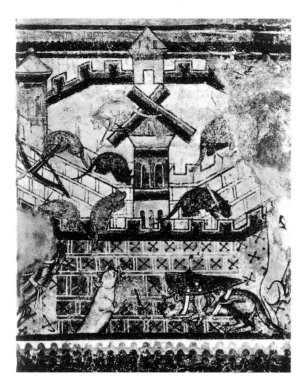

Mural, Johanneskapelle, Pürgg, Austria.

doubtless intended only to exemplify the maxim "make haste, slowly." The tortoise becomes the traditional symbol of the ponderous step of the sage.

The two fat cats shown assisting a particularly cantankerous and ungainly Saint Gertrude in an English caricature of 1782 are obviously there only for purposes of derision.[20] One can conclude that in the artists' heaven, cats have never been overendowed with the odor of sanctity.

Warrior Cats and Holy Wars

Cats' reputedly bellicose temperament—already we have witnessed their fierce wars against dogs—has given rise to some curious religious scenes.

One of the oldest is found in the mural of the Johanneskapelle in Purgg (Austria), executed in the mid-twelfth century (see p. 14).[21] In a very singular scene following an Annunciation, a Nativity and an Annunciation to the Shepherds, we see cats of warlike aspect, one bearing a long buckler on its back, mounting an assault on a fortress with crenellated ramparts, defended by mice, one of them armed with a powerful crossbow. No hint is given us as to the nature of the combat or the respective meanings of the two forces. But if this fortress is an allusion to the lovely biblical image "The Lord is my rock, and my fortress, and my deliverer" (Samuel II, 22:2), the feline attackers are once more blasphemers, with all due respect to Saint Gertrude and Saint Michael.

We must await the years—troubled, but rich in forceful images full of irony—of the Lutheran Reformation and the Counter-Reformation to see a cat fighting for a Christian cause. A Franciscan monk of Obernai, Thomas Murner (ca. 1475–1537), strongly opposed Luther, who in turn compared him to a wicked cat, grotesquely mad. The monk was dubbed, through a simple pun, "Murnarr"; "Narr" meant mad, and "Murr" and "Murner" are in fact old German words for tomcat.[22]

In reply, on the title page of his anti-Lutheran pamphlet *Von dem grossen lutherischen Narren* (Of the Great Lutheran Fool) Murner placed a woodcut that shows Murner himself as a cat-monk, trampling a fool on the ground—Luther, dressed in Augustine robes.[23] With the aid of a kind of phylactery, Murner extracts from his unhappy adversary's mouth tiny fool-figures, which disperse into the air (see p. 14).

By means of a play on words (sanctified for once), the cat is placed on the Catholic side in a curious allegorical composition of the early seventeenth century, entitled *Peace Exhorting the Churches to Harmony* (Utrecht, Rijksmuseum Het Catharijneconvent, see p. 15).[24] It is a Dutch picture inspired by an anonymous sixteenth-century engraving, urging tolerance in that era of violent religious conflict between Catholics and Protestants in the Low Countries. The figure of Peace approaches three people seated around a table for a meal. The guest's respective inscriptions supply puns that indicate their surprising attributes. At left, Calvin has before him a plate of veal (*calf* in Dutch recalls the sound of the reformer's name, whence one gets *calf fijn ist,* or "Calvinist"). Luther plays the lute (for "Lutheran"); in the center a Pope sits enthroned, holding a porringer of gruel (*pap,* gruel in Dutch, is very close to *paap,* that is, "Papist" in the same tongue). The two plump cats with round, sympathetic yellow eyes evoke the Catholics (*Catte lecken,* that is, "the cats lick"—for "Katholicken").

As will become clear in the section on secular emblematic images,

Of the Great Lutheran Fool, woodcut depicting Murner as a cat trampling Luther, Strasbourg, 1522.

the most superficial puns sometimes indicate, almost as an after-thought, completely unsuspected explanations. Thus one finds profound speculation in simple witticisms and mild rhetorical flourishes.

It was an abbott—the Italian Ferdinando Galiani (1728–1787)—who gave us the last word on the cat's eschatological destiny. Galiani, who was also a writer, economist and philosopher, became a devotee of the city's literary salons during a sojourn to Paris and knew Diderot well. In a letter, he shared with Mme. d'Épinay his plan to write a work entitled *A Mother Cat's Moral and Political Instructions to Her Young*, "Translated from Cat to French by M. D'Egrattigny [Mr. Scratchy], interpreter of the Cat language, for the King's Library."[25] The heroine of this story was to be the abbott's own cat, who "at first teaches her little ones to fear the human Gods. Then she explains theology to them and the two principles—the benevolent man God and the evil dog-demon; then she teaches them about ethics, the war on rats and on sparrows, etc.; finally she tells them about life beyond, in heavenly Ratapolis, which is a town in which the fortified walls are of Parmesan cheese [here the epistle-writer betrays his Italian origins], the floorboards of lights, the columns of eels, etc., and which is populated by altered cats, who are ordained, called to this state by the

Allegory of Sight, engraving by Jan Saenredam after Hendrik Goltzius.

The Excesses of Fashion, anonymous engraving, 1602.

man-God in order to be happy both in this world and the former, witness their plumpness, and they are excused from catching mice. Last, she counsels them to exhibit the most perfect resignation in the event that the man-God should call them to this state of perfection."

THE CAT, EVIL AND GOOD: CATS IN SECULAR PAINTING

In traditional symbology and in the language of allegory, which have so much in common, images are often infinitely simpler than the ideas they convey by means of quite tenuous rhetorical associations.

The cat's physical characteristics (keenness of sight, swiftness of neck and paw, agility) and its "personality" traits (independence, hatred of dogs, immoderate fondness for mice and birds) are too well known not to earn it a prominent place in iconographic treatises. Thus we shall see the motif of the cat endowed with different, even contradictory meanings: the feline will cast its lot now on the side of Good, now Evil; it will often be active, sometimes just onlookers, but never harmless and rarely innocent.

Cats and Allegories

The allegory best suited to the cat's qualities is surely that of Sight: indeed, cats are noted for their piercing vision—they can see even at night, a talent shared by a distant relative, the lynx. Northern European engravers thus often make use of cats in their depictions of Sight. This includes such artists as Hendrik Hondius (1573–1650) and, above all, Jan Saenredam (the father of the townscape painter). In his celebrated 1616 engraving after Hendrik Goltzius (1558–1617), we see a wide-eyed cat lying in the foreground beside some sundials (see p. 16). Behind it a woman, perhaps Venus, regards herself in a mirror held by a winged Cupid, while an eagle (also associated with Sight, as it supposedly can stare straight into the sun without harm) soars heavenward. The allegory's meaning is complicated (there are, also other figures in the composition, including the painter at his easel). A second idea is superimposed—that of the vanity of feminine beauty and of earthly love. Another *Sight*, also after Goltzius, done in 1578 by Philippe Galle, depicts a cat at the feet of a woman who stands, mirror in hand, with an eagle at her side.[26]

But a tomcat (or more often, a coquettish female cat) contemplating itself in a mirror can in and of itself evoke Sight, as in the series on the Five Senses by Barent Fabritius (see p. 122). This is so even when it is held—contented or not—in a young woman's arms, if we may interpret Bacchiacca's disturbing effigy (see p. 57) as an allegory of Sight. (In another of this master's paintings, at Berlin-Dahlem, we see a lynx in an analogous situation: this is very likely a similar allegory.)

The connection between cat and mirror can, via an elision in the rhetoric of allegory, serve equally well in other depictions, such as that of Pride ("Superbia"), for instance, in *The Seven Deadly Sins* (Madrid, the Prado) by Hieronymous Bosch (about 1453–1516), in which a little tiger cat on the threshold of the door watches a woman who adjusts her headdress before a mirror held up by a wolf-headed demon.

As an attentive observer of woman at her dressing-table, the cat can easily slip into the role of advisor, even accomplice. A strange cat indeed is the animal in Pieter Wtewael's *Vanity* (see pp. 86–87), posed directly in front of a rich mirror in which a young woman, courted by an elegant companion, regards her own sad reflection. It is certainly not the last time that a cat will be implicated, more or less directly, in the theme of Vanity.

In an early seventeenth-century German emblem book we once more find a cat in front of a mirror, regarding itself complacently (see p. 16). Nearby, a man dressed in the most foolish extreme of fashion seeks to capture someone's admiration. The accompanying commentary does not allude to an allegory of Sight; rather, it contains thoughts on aping outward appearances, the follies of fashion and the dangers inherent in over-fondness of novelty.[27]

As cats show a pronounced taste for independence, Cesare Ripa (ca. 1560–1620/1625) could not but associate one (a bit laboriously) with the idea (or better, the image) of Liberty—thus reviving a long tradition.[28] He wrote, "Liberty. The figure is a woman dressed in white, a scepter in her right hand, a cap in her left, and a cat close by her. . . . A cat is placed at her feet because there is no animal that loves freedom as does this one, which cannot bear any sort of confinement: because of which, some people, especially the Burgundians, carried it of old as a device on their war banners."[29]

The same idea figures in a late sixteenth-century German engraving, which depicts a cat bounding through a door: the legend explains that, of old, Germany's renown stemmed from the preference for death over loss of liberty.[30]

Must we, for all that, interpret the cat's presence in the studio of Velázquez' *Weavers* (see pp. 94–95) as an allusion to the freedoms enjoyed under the liberal reign of the Spanish monarchy, as others have done for years? We leave to J. H. de Azcárate the responsibility for this ingenious but extremely speculative interpretation.[31]

It cannot be denied, however, that the cat has a part in monarchist iconography: witness the oval bas-relief of Liberty executed in 1784 by Nicolas Beauvalet (1750–1818) for the bedchamber of Louis XVI at the Château de Compiègne (see p. 17). An interesting and traditional interpretation, it must be seen within the larger context of a liberty indeed cherished by the king, a liberty that prospered and maintained itself under his protection. On the medallion is a delicately sculpted woman in classical dress, with a dignified Greek profile, holding a club (like that of Hercules) with which she has broken the yoke that lies at her feet. On a rock that serves as a pedestal, a cat, also with a Grecian profile, faces the woman.[32]

The existence of such a royal-liberal cat refutes the recent analysis by Margaret Armbrust Seibert,[33] who, with Théophile Gautier and Champfleury, sees the cat as a typically republican symbol of the French Revolution borrowed over the centuries from the iconography of the virtuous Roman republic. In actuality, the Revolution's iconography—even in the case of the cat—did nothing but adopt for its own purposes the emblems that had but lately served the disgraced monarchy.

Be that as it may, less than fifteen months after having presided over the king's slumber at Compiègne, the cat had offered its services to the new French Constitution, "founded by wisdom upon the immutable basis of the rights of man and the duties of a citizen," according to an engraving exhibited at the 1798 Salon by Pierre-Paul Prud'hon (1758–1823). In it, a corpulent cat sits at the feet of Liberty, who tramples the yoke and broken chains. She holds a staff topped with a Phrygian cap; flanking her are Minerva, the Law (with the heraldic cock and a lamb paired with a lion) and Nature (accompanied

Nicolas Beauvalet, Liberty, bas-relief, 1784, Compiègne, Musée national du Château.

Pierre-Paul Prud'hon, The French Constitution, engraving exhibited in the Paris Salon of 1798.

Left: Cornelis Cornelisz van Haarlem, Charity (detail), Valenciennes, Musée des Beaux-Arts.

Right: Cat Clawing a Child in Defense of Its Young, anonymous sixteenth-century painting, Musée de Saumur-en-Auxois.

by children), whom the cat faces (see p. 17).

When one speaks of cats, one speaks of quick movement. Thus Paris Nogari (ca. 1536–1601) has depicted Swiftness in a fresco that adorns the old Chamber of the Swiss Guards in the Vatican.[34] Cesare Ripa cites other examples of allegories that employ cats. Contrast ("Contrasto") is depicted as a man in armor, holding an sword, between a cat and a dog who confront each other, antagonists by their very natures. We also suggest that a *contrario* may be seen in the enigmatic sixteenth-century Italian portrait of a young man (see p. 56) holding a cat and dog that are in perfect amity, as an allegory for the harmony between the contradictory elements of human nature. The figure of enmity ("Inimicitia") is also accompanied by a cat and dog— for the same, rather simplistic reasons as in *Contrast*—and is joined by an eel, since eels reputedly flee all other fish.[35]

The last allegory is even more complex: it is Persuasion ("Persuasione"), who holds on a leash an animal with three heads—a dog's, a cat's and a monkey's.[36] According to Ripa, the animals' presence can be explained thus: the cat, by its innate alertness, will incite the listener to attentiveness in his turn; the dog, which knows how to flatter and caress out of self-interest, is there to win good will; as for the monkey, reputedly the best at understanding human thought, it is perfectly able to impress the object of persuasion. We are not too surprised to learn that this last allegory, at once complicated and esthetically inharmonious, did not enjoy tremendous success among artists.

In other instances the cat, without representing, properly speaking, the principle within an allegory, may serve to reinforce its meaning. Thus the cat that hurls itself upon a giant ham bone on a plate in the foreground of *Intemperence* by Jan Steen (1626–1679) cannot but reemphasize the many excesses to which the various guests in the scene abandon themselves. Not far from the cat, the symbols of vanity (a clock, a broken glass) remind us of the transience of worldly pleasures (Private Collection).

Equally significant is the cat in a strange painting by Jan Miense Molenaer (ca. 1610–1668). Beside a table bearing, pell-mell, the usual trappings of Vanity (a skull, glasses, playing cards and musical instruments) a dwarf stands smoking a pipe; on the other side of the table sits a little cat (see p. 19). It appears to emphasize, by its fleetness, the implacable flight of Time.[37] Molenaer also painted a cat, playing with young children, but this animal is not harmless either (see p. 102). The moral of the story is clear: just as earthly joys pass, the children's play may be interrupted at any moment by a scratch.

About a century and a half later, Prud'hon also placed two children in a composition entitled *The Blow of the Cat's Paw* (sketch at the Musée Fabre in Montpellier). An ironical Cupid, trampling his quiver and arrows, holds a cat that has just scratched a little girl, who cries with pain. The picture's pendant, *Love Caresses Before Wounding*, shows the same two children playing with a puppy. Whereas the dog is faithful and harmless, the cat lets fly with cruel claws; love's pleasures do not go without torments. Prud'hon's acquaintance with traditional iconography is indeed apparent, but his recourse to the facile image of the cat's claw is no less meaningful for all that.

Another "allegorical" blow of the paw—one that gained fame early in the artist's life—is that in Cornelis van Haarlem's *Charity* (see p. 18).[38] Van Mander, the Vasari of the Northern schools, describes it in his *Het Schilder-Boeck*, published in 1604: "A Charity, under the features of a seated woman, has near her a few children one of whom has seized a cat that seems to mew and claw him on the thigh. The child's pain was extraordinarily well-rendered . . . " The cat, its tail disproportionately long, could not be a "gratuitous" motif, dear to the adherents of a certain, purely anecdotal Northern realism. May not it indicate, very simply, the limits of charity's benefits? Into this harmonious, optimistic world of optimistic charity, which ultimately relies on man's goodness, is interjected a negative and pessimistic note of instinctive wickedness and aggression, which is no less a part of nature than is virtue.

Let us note that Frans Floris also painted a plump cat at the feet of one of the children that surround Charity (Leningrad, Hermitage). But this feline is very peaceful and harmless, proof that the connection between the cat and Charity could be interpreted differently by artists who were contemporaries, and what's more, of the same school. In complete contrast is the enormous cat attacking a grimacing *putto* in the rather uncanny painting at the Musée de Saumur-en-Auxois (see p. 18). What is the subject of this anonymous composition (are we sure that it is a fragment?), of which we know neither the exact school (Italian?) nor its date (sixteenth century?). Perhaps it is an allegory of parental love: the cat only claws the child because the latter has taken its kittens. Cats defending their young against dogs, as we shall see, were in fact popular images of parents' love for their children. The picture at Saumur transposes this into the scholarly language of allegory.

Jan Miense Molenaer, Vanity with Dwarf and Cat, Private Collection.

Cats, Proverbs, Emblems, and Popular Wisdom

A domestic pet *par excellence*, the cat was perpetual grist for the pleasant images of the language of so-called popular wisdom. The best examples of its use for moralistic purposes may be found in the derisive culture of the Netherlands and Germany—in both painting and, more

Illustrations from a collection of proverbs by Jacob Cats, 1712 edition, Amsterdam.

often, in prints, which were particularly well suited to the diffusion of ideas.[39]

"Belling the cat" is both hazardous (the cat may actively protest) and senseless (wearing so clangorous an ornament, the unfortunate animal henceforth will be unable to pursue the rodents that raid the granaries). Thus a veritable buffoon attempts this ridiculous task, wearing the traditional clothes of his state, in Sebastian Brandt's famous *Ship of Fools* (*Das Narrenschiff*), published in Basel in 1494 and illustrated in many later versions.[40] In the work by Pieter Brueghel the Elder (ca. 1525/1530–1569), the beller, crazier than ever, has donned a coat of armor to escape the cat's claws, and another idea presents itself—that arms lend a coward courage (see pp. 72–73).

A woodcut dated 1558, with a Dutch legend, depicts a fool confronted with a cat that perches on his shoulder, licking his face, while its hind paws claw him.[41] The moral: one should mistrust those who flatter one openly and then stab one in the back.

"An old cat does not play ball," according to another old saw. So we see in a drawing by Jacob Jordaens (1593–1678), which shows several people seated at a table and trying in vain to tease a cat into playing (Musée du Louvre, Cabinet des dessins). This feline, independent and sensible like an old sage, does not permit its conduct to be thus dictated or influenced.

Consulted by generations of artists and immensely famous in its day was the copious collection of proverbs first published in The Hague in 1632 by the Dutchman Jacob Cats. It was a compilation of the sayings of all the European nations in their original languages, linking them through simple word-plays or via congruity between ideas.[42] The painter Adriaen Pietersz van de Venne (1589–1662) did the drawings for the engravings that illustrate the principle sayings. A number of these allude to cats, and in each the relationship between the animal and the moral of the story is laboriously spelled out.

Thus the cat that busily licks a candle, near a young man who courts a stout, awkward woman, demonstrates to what depths a greedy suitor will stoop (see p. 20). Since the woman will inherit a rich farm, the young dowry-hunter must pretend to find her beautiful, just as the cat forces itself to lick the candle that it actually detests.[43] Let us note that Jacob Cats's parallels are occasionally surprisingly farfetched.

"If a cat snoops, hit it on the muzzle,"[44] advises a French saying (the English would say, "Curiosity killed the cat"). In the illustration, a woman uses some tongs to drive away a cat that has crept too close to a container warming on the hearth (see p. 20). The moral: he who is too curious receives well-deserved buffets for which he has only himself to blame.

"If one owns a pretty cat," they say, "it's best to avoid the furrier."[45] A man of that trade sneaks up on a cat, intending to capture it, as a couple strolls by in the background (see p. 21). Like the young girl, who risks being courted solely for her looks, the cat is sought after only for its fur.

According to an Italian proverb, it is foolish to let a tomcat lick the spit that's been used to cook a roast: if a good watch is not kept, the animal will go on to eat the entire piece of meat.[46] That seems just about to happen in the scene illustrating this proverb, if the two people present should leave the room. But the shrewd young woman will not do so; similarly, according to the wisdom of the time, it was often considered wise to chaperone young women.

Another woman, in a seventeenth-century engraving entitled *She Lets the Cat at the Cheese,* is courted by a young man[47]; a cat meanwhile takes advantage of her distraction to climb up on the table and devour the cheese, rather oddly not preventing a rat from nibbling the food as well. "A bon chat, bon rat," the saying goes, and the cat thus assures itself a future repast. The young woman reveals herself to be extremely calculating as well in encouraging a suitor from whom she hopes to profit.

Another cat, says Cats, had become so unbearable that the mistress of the house asked her husband to get rid of it.[48] In Van de Venne's medallion of the scene, the man, armed with an sword, seems to be attacked by the cat, and the room has been reduced to a shambles (see p. 21). The cat, while threatened, has become as fierce as a lion, and the human warrior must give up his attempts to kill it. Thus some enterprises, no matter how necessary, must be abandoned. Man cannot always carry out all that he wishes.

The motif of a cat that is seized with extraordinary courage when threatened by man is employed in an early seventeenth-century German engraving to illustrate another idea—that of the energy of despair. In the engraving an unhappy cat, surrounded by some men armed with sticks, must hurl itself into their midst if it would escape.[49]

The theme of the war between cats and rats or mice has obviously inspired the most proverbs and fables. In this battle, the cat often plays the villain. La Fontaine, for example, created for all eternity a hypocritical, underhanded, sly beast: "a smug cat, plush-furred, big and fat," a "pious one," a "tartuffe" (the term used in the fable *The Cat and the Fox*)—these are the poor animal's attributes. In this truly detestable light, as simplistic as it is inexact, was the cat represented for years to young children during their first years of education.[50]

Popular morality was expressed in several wise sayings, among them this well-known one: "When you deny nature, it comes back in a hurry!" A late sixteenth-century engraving shows a cat atop a table, catching a mouse under the eyes of a serious assembly as if it were assisting with a scientific experiment (see p. 22).[51] Even if it had wanted to, the cat could not have resisted its natural leaning—that is, to chase mice: no one can go against his fundamental inclinations, the commentary emphasizes. Jacob Cats's work includes an illustration of the same type. In it, monkeys delouse a child while some cats chase mice. An observer explains it all to his young companion: just as cats know no other endeavor but chasing mice, and monkeys fleas, lovelorn men never weary of seeking out wives. The true nature of each must one day emerge.[52] La Fontaine's fable *The Cat Metamorphosed into a Woman* (Book II, fable XL) takes up this theme as well: "so powerful is nature" that, at the mere sight of a mouse, the woman rediscovers her feline instincts.

Illustrations from a collection of proverbs by Jacob Cats, 1712 edition, Amsterdam.

An indefatigable mouse-hunter, the cat serves to illustrate many other adages, even the most surprising. One of Cats's proverbs is illustrated with the image of a man who proudly marches along with some cats, holding on his shoulder a pike with dead rats skewered upon it (see p. 22).[53] The motto: "He who hunts with cats will catch only rats." He who hunts with cats, not dogs, will bag only what cats can catch: rats or mice, but nothing else. By the same token, each must be assigned the tasks that suit his talents; one must not entrust servants with things beyond their powers.

Hunting mice in order to keep them from eating grain is a noble pursuit. But, as a mid-sixteenthth-century engraving from Antwerp illustrates,[54] the cat may fail in its duty and be tempted to steal forbidden food. Indeed, the cat on the left eyes the table, while another escapes at right with its pilfered meal. Some gibbets in the background

German engraving illustrating the saying, "When you deny nature, it comes back in a hurry," 1596.

Illustration from a collection of proverbs by Jacob Cats, 1712 edition, Amsterdam.

announce the future punishment. Just as the thieving cat risks betraying itself by purring, the commentary explains, so the imprudent malefactor will be unmasked and punished by hanging. And if the misdeed remains hidden at first, the punishment to come will be doubly severe.

Cats were much in demand as ratters, and a lively commerce grew up around supplying proven rodent-catchers to households in need of them. A seventeenth-century German engraving by Gerhard Altzenbach, much more elaborate than the preceding one, bears the motto *Katz im Sack*, which is analogous to the French proverb about "selling a cat in a bag." It shows a charlatan selling felines in just that way.[55] *Caveat emptor.* His dupes, in buying a cat without first inspecting it, have no means of knowing what kind of beast it is. Let us buy nothing with our eyes closed; and in the same way, let us mistrust appearances in choosing a companion or mate, mindful of the seductive masks each may wear.

A cat leaving to hunt mice with, in the foreground, a warrior, in an early seventeenth-century German emblem warns soldiers against pillaging.[56] The voraciousness of the cat, which kills more mice than it can eat, symbolizes the greedy imprudence of the soldier who, in his turn, risks being surprised by the enemy retracing its steps.

In the seventeenth century, the theme of the cat and the mousetrap far surpassed in popularity the relatively limited world of proverbs. To Northern European painters, the mousetrap was both a picturesque object and a symbol easily understood by all. With or without a cat nearby, it embodied the basic idea of Love which ensnares. "He is caught who thought to capture." Thus an unhappy mouse has been ensnared in trying to gain a morsel of lard, as Cats shows.[57] The parallel is a simple one: like the animal, the lover becomes a prisoner; and according to Cats the rodent that tries to take the food without being caught represents a dishonorable lover who would seduce a young woman without marrying her.[58]

An early seventeenth-century Dutch engraving depicts a cat eyeing a mouse that cowers inside an open trap, while a little Cupid watches them both.[59] A text inspired by a Petrarch sonnet explains the scene: if the mouse remains in its trap, it is in certain peril, but if it leaves, it faces death once more, as the cat awaits this very event in order to pounce. Thus, we must conclude, there is no hope of salvation outside the chains of love.

Several works by Abraham Mignon (1640–1679) illustrate this theme. In one, at the foot of a vase either balanced or just beginning to fall (perhaps a symbol of Vanity), a cat caterwauls fiercely beside an upside-down mousetrap in which hides a terrified mouse (Leningrad, Hermitage; and Lyons, Musée des Beaux-Arts). The cat's fury bears witness to its frustration and, more profoundly, to the vanity of its aims.

In the same vein, Philips Angel (1616–1683) painted a cat watching a mouse (Rennes, Musée des Beaux-Arts). The mouse balances on a straw that comes from a vase lying on its side; the scene doubtless depicts the mousetrap of fate—if the mouse enters the mouth of the vase, the straw will shift, and the mouse will be caught inside. The rodent is not within the trap, but danger is nonetheless imminent.

A painting (sometimes attributed to Bachelier) executed a century later depicts a magnificent, ruffed Angora watching a mouse caught in a trap (see p. 23). To one side, three adorable kittens in a round basket seem more interested in a bowl of milk: one would like to say that they represent the innocence of childhood. But the work is eighteenth-century, and its decorative and narrative elements override its

symbolic meaning. Its primary focus, rather, is the *trompe-l'oeil*, in the background, in which we see some hooks upon which hangs a key. If the Age of Reason hadn't been slightly superficial—at least with regard to painting—one would be tempted to interpret the key (the key to freedom), so important in the composition, as an additional allusion to the non-freedom of Love. From time to time, children can act as intermediaries, even go-betweens, for cat and mouse: thus, in 1676 Adriaen der Werff (1659–1722) painted two children, one holding a cat and the other an intricate mousetrap in which a mouse has been caught (London, art market)[60]; the same artist painted a young boy taking a dead mouse from a trap designed not only to catch but to kill, and offering the mouse to a cat (London, National Gallery).[61] There the murderous trap no longer permits the lover even a choice between captivity and death.

The theme of a dead mouse offered to a cat enjoyed great popularity among the Dutch, especially among masters of the *manière fine* (the *fijnschilders*) of 1650 to 1700, from Gerrit Dou (1613–1675) to Pieter van Slingerland (1640–1691) and Willem van Mieris (1662–1747).[62] The subject was later incorporated, without its symbolic meaning, into genre scenes, such as Martin Drolling's *Woman with a Mousetrap* (see pp. 166–67).

In other cases, in an understandable parallel, the mouse and trap were replaced by a bird in a cage, but the meaning of the cat's presence remained the same. Hendrik van der Neer executed several paintings of this type (see p. 123)[63]; in one (Brunswick, Herzog Anton Ulrich-Museum),[64] a statue of Venus seems to watch over two children who play with a bird, a cage and a cat, thus replacing the earlier symbolic motif of Cupid, who presided over the Dutch engravings at the beginning of the century, cited earlier.

Other animals—the lion, for instance—are also pitted against the cat. An early seventeenth-century German engraving[65] shows how dangerous it can be to provoke someone stronger than oneself: the cat who plays with the lion's tail is as imprudent as a small nation that teases and aggravates a mighty prince.

The dog, which is the cat's traditional foe in religious paintings and secular allegories, remains so in popular iconography. At least once, though, the two species' incompatibility inspired a very early seventeenth-century German engraving that depicts the innate love parents feel for their children.[66] In it, two cats, claws flying, protect their kittens from a dog, putting it to flight.

Such laudable motives are absent from a confrontation between cat and dog shown in a painting by Paulus Potter (1625–1654) executed

23

*Bertrand and Raton before a trompe-l'oeil fireplace,
eighteenth-century French painting, Paris, Private Collection.*

*Monkey and Cat, anonymous eighteenth-century painting,
Paris, Mobilier national, depository of the Musée du Louvre.*

in 1652 and now entitled *Like Cats and Dogs*, a well-chosen if apocryphal title (Bentinck-Thyssen Collection).[67]

In an illustration of the popular theme of domestic discord, dear to the imagery of Épinal, cat and dog confront one another again, each taking the part of one member of the couple. The dog sides with the wife, cat with the husband (see p. 23).[68] The text clarifies each's role: "the dog who yelps and bites, / Barks to restore accord. / The cat who scratches and tears one's clothes / Does it all for the tailor's profit." The wicked cat once more plays the part of disturber of the peace, and the dog represents order.

The next most frequent pairing is of a monkey and a cat, a juxtaposition unfavorable to the latter, as the monkey is reputed to be the cleverest of the animals. One thinks immediately of La Fontaine's fable *The Monkey and the Cat* (Book IX, fable 176), inspired by Aesop and Phaedrus (see Hondius, p. 119); Landseer, p. 175; and Decamps, p. 174). The story is simple. A monkey (Bertrand) persuades the cat (Raton) that no one else in all the world can match Raton at pulling chestnuts from the fire. The flattered feline begins to do so, and its paws are burnt more or less badly depending on the painter's adherence to a cruel realism. As for the monkey, it devours the chestnuts as they emerge. La Fontaine's moral is that some princes, won over by their sovereign's flattery, are prepared to do anything the king asks, for his profit alone.

An eighteenth-century French painting (see p. 24),[69] rather naive but full of zest, depicts the two playmates in front of a *trompe-l'oeil* chimney (one can see the bellows and tongs to each side). The artist has made use of the fact that the scene must necessarily take place near a hearth (a true iron stove in Landseer's work, a traditional fireplace in Decamps's) to depict one on the firescreen, of the sort that were so popular in the eighteenth century, and of which we have a celebrated example by François Desportes, *Dog at Its Bowl* (1751), which adorns a fireplace at the Musée de la Vénerie in Senlis.

At times the dialogue between cat and monkey explodes into furious conflict. An anonymous eighteenth-century (French?) painting depicts a cat violently attacking a monkey that is stealing the cat's young; a child in a large plumed hat watches with amusement (Paris, Musée du Louvre, see p. 24).[70] In mid-eighteenth-century art the picturesque decidedly overrides the symbolic: one would otherwise like to see in this work a last representation, in an exotic mode (a monkey instead of a dog), of the old theme of cats' affection for their progeny, which was so prevalent at the dawn of the previous century.

Cats, Jests and Sorcery

The theme of an absurd world, in which values are turned upside down, in which the weak win out over the strong, animals play human roles or vice-versa, or in which, within the animal kingdom, the perennial hunters become the hunted, the predators are devoured—in short, a topsy-turvy world—has always fired artists' imaginations. The cat could not help but play a large part in this reversal of roles and, of course, its primary arena is the eternal struggle between cats and rats or mice.[71] Although the cats of ancient Egypt are outside of the scope of this work, we cannot help but include the whimsical spirit that, in spite of the cult devoted to cats, once inspired an artist on the banks of the Nile to depict Lady Mouse having her hair done by a cat, and Master Tomcat caring for some baby ducklings.[72]

Many of the engravings illustrating late sixteenth- and early seventeenth-century German emblem books employ the inexhaustible theme of a captive cat mocked by mice. In one of these, two cats are imprisoned in cages about which mice dance unrestrainedly (see p. 25).[73] The accompanying text explains that the mice, a fearful race, are making the most of the cats' captivity; in the same way, the effrontery of a nation that is certain of its own impunity knows no bounds. Another such scene attempts to put mice (and men as well) on their guard, as the cat may suddenly bound forth from its trap, and mete out harsh retribution.[74]

David Teniers the Younger (1610–1690) takes up this theme in one of his paintings (see p. 25).[75] The cat is not caged, but its situation is no better for that: a peasant woman is holding it in her lap to delouse it, as the mice scamper up to savor the spectacle of their immobilized enemy. But they should beware the moment when, rid of its fleas, the cat bounds back into the farmyard.

Another cat, seen through seventeenth-century Italian eyes, is indeed caged (see p. 26). Some rats, one holding a little flag, tease the cat by running right up next to the cage, while other rats jingle tiny bells as if inviting the onlookers to enjoy the spectacle. All the while, the people (dressed as actors) who watch the scene smile in a rather disturbing fashion. The rats really ought to make sure that one of these people does not amuse himself by suddenly freeing the cat.

"A bon chat, bon rat" is the title of an engraving published in Paris in about 1640. In it a surprising scene unfolds.[76] A cat nurses some

"The cats are prisoners, the mice dance,"
German engraving, 1565.

David Teniers the Younger, Peasant Woman Delousing a Cat,
Private Collection.

baby rats; next to it another rat feeds kittens from a spoon. The moral of the topsy-turvy situation is this: in nursing the little rats, the cat fattens its future prey; as for the rat, it hopes by feeding gruel to the young cats to conciliate future generations of felines. But cats will never give up eating rats.

In popular imagery throughout the centuries, up until the famous Épinal images, which reached their apogee in 1860, this recurrent theme was depicted with never-ending delight. Side by side with the hen that pecks at a fox's back, the horse that mounts its rider, the bear that forces its master to dance, and the hare or pig that roasts the cook on a spit, we see the rat taunting the imprisoned cat, or the mice that chase or even eat it. In other scenes a tomcat (or, more often, a female cat) will sit in rapt self-contemplation before its mistress's mirror, while she chases after mice on all fours. Or a woman will crawl about a kitchen in search of mice, under the dignified gaze of feline chefs— if they do not actually offer her a dead mouse.[77]

In a seventeenth-century painting of the Italian school, several cats holding a food market (one weighs lard with a scale) serve a man

Captive Cat and Mice Celebrating, anonymous seventeenth-century painting, Art market.

Cats Holding a Market, seventeenth-century Italian painting.

with a child (see p. 26).[78] Behind them, a hatted brigand straight out of a Caravaggio canvas prepares to steal some money, or perhaps tries to take hold of a cat. Although the work's subject is unknown—it may illustrate a scene from the Commedia dell'Arte—it perfectly fits the burlesque milieu in which animals pursue human occupations.

This idea also suffuses numerous pictures of children who treat a cat like a living doll. They teach it to read or dance (see Steen, pp. 120–21); in a painting by Jacopo Amigoni (1682–1752), they make it eat with a spoon, to which the cat, its eyes strangely luminous, submits with a bad grace (Aurillac, Musée des Beaux-Arts). Similarly, the English artist Joseph Wright of Derby painted a kitten being dressed up as a doll by laughing children (see p. 164).

At times people treat cats as they would their own children, as in the scene said to depict Candlemas and attributed to Niccolo Frangipani (1555–1600). In it, some rather tipsy people surround a swaddled cat and feed it gruel (Nantes, Musée des Beaux-Arts).[79] The tableau stems from an old Candlemas custom in which people gave cats gruel in a parody of Saint Joseph feeding the Infant Jesus.

The great Watteau (1684–1721), in a painting that has been lost but survives in an engraving, speaks to the allied theme of the ailing cat. In a scene perhaps inspired by Italian comedy, a doctor takes a feline's pulse as a young woman tries to keep it quiet. The legend of the engraving, by Jean-Michel Liotard (1731), criticizes the excessive love some women show for their cats; it goes on to say they would look "with joy upon a lover's death." As for the doctor, "If he applied his uncertain skills only to cats / What happiness 'twould be for the human race!"

Doctors and apothecaries also busy themselves about a sick cat in a work by Faustino Bocchi (see p. 148), but here we quit the confines of the human theater for the painter's fantastical, grotesque world in which most of the people are dwarves and the animals are giants. This reversal and the scene's absurdity induce a feeling of malaise that Bocchi plays on, mocking humans through the medium of animals.[80]

Equally ironic and burlesque by definition, the paintings known as *singeries* depict monkeys dressed up as important people and involved in all kinds of activities. Equally well-dressed cats frequently mingle with this peculiar company. A particularly odd theme, the "monkeys of the guard corps," was given a picturesque rendition by David Teniers the Younger, which met with immediate success and was often copied (see p. 27).[81] In a shadowy room, military monkeys gather, playing cards, gossiping or smoking; some put on proud musketeers' airs, others wear strange receptacles as helmets. The door has just opened to admit a cat, dressed in a striped tunic; gripped by two armed guards, it has just been arrested. We do not know of what offence it is guilty; according to the author of an eighteenth-century catalogue that describes a similar painting, the cat is a spy. The fanatical Swiss cat painter Gottfried Mind (1768–1814) executed an engraving after Teniers's painting, in which the prisoner, dressed in a skirt and blouse, is a female cat—what is more, a female cat of easy virtue.[82] In another painting, more or less based on that of Teniers, two cats are brought before a military tribunal of monkeys (Paris, Musée du Louvre).[83] In these scenes (more satirical than moralistic) it falls to the monkeys, little mock-men, to impose order in a land where, yet again, the cat signifies trouble and perturbation.

A more peaceful scene, the famous "monkey barbers," also derives from Teniers the Younger. In a hairdresser's salon, run by monkeys loaded down with bottles of all descriptions, a cat is having its whiskers curled with a small iron. The monkey has donned glasses, the better to see what it is doing: the cat sits quietly, on its knees a mirror—an object previously associated more seriously with cats in Vanitas images—in which it will soon be able to admire its finished hairstyle.[84]

Parodic animal concerts, the expressions of a completely imaginary universe whose ultimate source is the fantastic bestiary of the Middle Ages, were a favorite subject of painters, particularly Northern artists, as a work by Teniers the Younger (again!) bears witness (see p. 115). Of course, the word *Kattenmusik* in Flemish and Dutch (like the German *Katzenmusik*) means a loud din. The cat is thus in an excellent position to participate in the rudely cacaphonous musical assemblies in which, ironically, monkeys are guests.[85] *Concerts miauliques* were very popular in France as well, and many engravings depicted these ludicrous events. In one, a music teacher surrounded by cats, some reading from scores entitled "Mi Mi Miaou," boasts of his talents: "You who don't know the worth of Music, / Come listen to the magnificent concert, / And the ravishing airs that I teach the Tomcats. /Since my lovely voice soothes the savage beasts, / I will not fail to instruct every one of you, / nor to enlighten you as to the difficult notes."[86] Another satiric engraving, doubtless an allusion to

inferior musicians—who, as everyone knows, are quite common, but who are oblivious to their shortcomings—depicts an Academy of Music with the commentary: "To cure your headache, / Or just to have a lark, / Leave off of human music, / Come to the Cats' Opera. / To the strains of the *concert miaulique*, / If old Orpheus arrived, / He who made all the world dance to his music, / He himself would dance today."[87]

As strange as it may seem, the motif of cats gathered about a musical score has also been linked with the perennial battle between cats and mice. In fact, there are engravings—including one by Dunker, after a Jan Brueghel painting—that depict an assembly of cats in front of a very singular music book[88] in which the notes are replaced by little black and white mice whose tails indicate the eighth- and sixteenth-notes.

In beating time, the cats scratch the unhappy rodents trapped in the staves, which probably explains the feline musicians' verve. In his famous book *Les Chats*, Champfleury tells of having seen a firescreen of this kind in his youth; it was an amusing memory.

Eighteenth-century France was mad on animal concerts, more for decorative than allegorical reasons; the fashion of wooden panels ornamented with *singeries* (Watteau, Gillot, Audran, Berain, Peyrotte) reached its zenith.[89] Thus we see cats dancing in an engraving after Jean-Baptiste Oudry (1686–1755), or playing the drum or guitar in a

David Teniers the Younger, The Monkeys of the Guard Corps, The Hague, Dienst Verspreide Rijkscollecties.

*Hans Baldung Grien, Witches at a Sabbath,
Musée du Louvre, Cabinet des dessins.*

*Saint Aelwaer, woodcut, ca. 1550, Amsterdam,
Rijksmuseum, Rijksprentenkabinet.*

composition by Christophe Huet (?–1759) at the Musée des Arts décoratifs in Paris.

It remains to chronicle the scenes of witchcraft—born of the populace's horrid superstitions—in which cats, to their sorrow, possess citizens' rights. Since cats—especially black cats—were considered witches' obligatory companions, they were often chased and slaughtered. Curiously, the traditional iconographic repertoire is rather deceptive in this regard.[90] If one established an order of rank of cats in early paintings, the Annunciation, the Last Supper and the Supper at Emmaus would come long before the scenes of the witches' sabbath. In fact, the cat is not always present in these last, and when it is, it is rarely alone, most often sharing the malefic festivities with strange billy-goats, night birds (barn owls or horned owls), bats, and reptiles of all kinds.

In spite of this, several famous "sorcerer" cats exist: one by Hans Baldung Grien (1484/1485–1545)[91] is preserved in the Louvre's Cabinet des dessins (see p. 28); some may be seen in engravings by Jacques de Gheyn (1565–1629) and Gillot (1673–1722); and of course there are several rather sinister felines in the *Caprichos* of Goya (1746–1828). Alessandro Magnasco (1667–1749) several times painted witches surrounded by small silhouettes that can only be cats emerging from the gloom,[92] but Magnasco's cats are everywhere; they appear just as often at the feet of monks or nuns. It was the nineteenth century that lent the sorceress or fortune-teller and her cat their most characteristic stamp, as, for example, a striking, almost unknown painting, *The Tarot Reader* by Clémentine Dondey (ca. 1813–?) in which a black cat of absolutely diabolical aspect perches upon its dour mistress's shoulder (see p. 29). Notably, in certain Tarot decks a menacing clawed cat appears on the card of Treason. Paul Ranson's 1893 *The Sorceress and the Cat* is a completely stereotyped version of the theme, and is only rescued from banality by its decorative, streamlined Nabi style (see p. 191).

A more interesting figure by far is "Saint" Aelwaer, a sort of demonic anti-saint, patroness of all tribulation, depicted in a 1550 engraving by the Dutch artist Cornelis Anthonisz (ca. 1499–1553).[93] Grimacing and querulous, Aelwaer sits upon an ass (this lowly animal is often the mount of the fool), holding a pig, symbol of gluttony and laziness, and brandishing, like an ensign, a cat that harks back yet again to the forces of evil (see p. 28). The magpie perched on Aelwaer's head calls to mind the indiscreet prattle and immorality to which this termagant abandons herself. An intemperate cavalier, mother of all vices, Aelwaer is a sort of Virgin Mary in reverse, which is why, mounted on her donkey, she recalls the image of Mary fleeing into Egypt with the Infant Jesus. The magpie, etched against a "halo" that is actually not a halo, is a mocking allusion to the dove of the Holy Spirit, which descended upon the Virgin and the apostles at Pentecost. This satirical image, which condemns the woman's looseness and her pleasure in profaning what is sacred, perfectly fits the tradition of the world upside down, in which wicked or forbidden images found expression under the guise of irrationality. It also, in the troubled, iconoclastic Reformation in the Netherlands, allowed artists to hold up to derision a medieval Christian iconography singularly weighed down with superstition.

Cats in Arms and At War

Cats' bellicose natures, which facilitated their inclusion in religious quarrels, also suited them to purely martial dramas.

Historically, felines first engaged in battle in ancient Persia, at the Siege of Pelusium in Egypt by King Cambyses: the poor animals were roped into it despite themselves. The painter Paul Lenoir (?–1881) created a flabbergasting "Oriental" evocation of the scene, which was exhibited at the Paris Salon of 1873 (see p. 29). "To vanquish the Egyptians' obstinate resistance, the Persian king resorted to a stratagem: after collecting all of the cats in the region, he launched a final assault, throwing these sacred animals before him . . . And the people of Pelusium, terrified, preferred to surrender their town rather than run the risk of killing or wounding their gods (525 B.C.)."[94] So, according to the Greek historian Polyen, the cruel, calculating Cambyses was said to have played on his enemies' religious beliefs in order to conquer Pelusium.

There are many other battles in which cats, representing the combatants of this or that epoch, participate indirectly in history. For example, we see dogs besieging a fortress of cats, the *Forteza de Gatte*, in a seventeenth-century Italian woodcut. In the background is a camp of mice who lend the dogs a helping hand.[95]

Here again, rats and mice are cats' inveterate enemies. The combatants are of many nationalities: they could be German, Dutch (the cats' stronghold is called "Katten-toorn") or English.[96] In this case, the combat is naval (English cats, mice, and rats would be a seafaring lot, obviously): a boat, the *Royal Rat*, from which the mice stream, attacks a coastal bastion, the "Cats' Castle." There were also French battles: in a popular engraving published in Lyon in 1610, the fortress of "Maistre Mitou, prince des Chatz" is surrounded by an army of rats.[97] The work's title, "The Great and Marvellous Battle Between the Cats and the Rats, or Between the Big Thieves and the Little Thieves" indicates a struggle between two extremely disreputable nations. Another seventeenth-century engraving, also French, depicts afresh the mice and rats banded together to storm the cats' fortress, in which the cats' prince and leader Raminagrobis is enthroned.[98] The rodents pour from all directions in close-ranked batallions; certain rats, the text specifies, arrive by sea from the "Isles of Moréciano cavero," an obvious reference to the mercenary soldiers so often called

Clémentine Dondey, The Tarot Reader, Dijon, Musée des Beaux-Arts.

Paul Lenoir, King Cambyses at the Siege of Pelusium, 1872, location unknown.

29

Quand les francois prendrons
ARRAS les Souris mengeront
les Chats, les francois on pris ARRAS
et si les Souris non poinct mange
les Chats

ARRAS Pris Par Les Francois Le 10 Aoust 1640

Jacques Lagniet, When the French took Arras . . . ,
seventeenth-century engraving depicting the siege of 1640
in which the French cats took the town of Arras,
which was defended by its inhabitants, the rats.

upon by warring parties. Spies from both camps, if captured, would be hanged on the spot.

One of the most celebrated of all feline wars is linked to a famous town in northern France—Arras. Yet again, from a simple play of words—"a rat" for "Arras"—an entire iconographic tradition was born.

Very early on, the bishop's and town's arms were adorned with rats. It was equally natural that the inhabitants of Arras should be identified with rats. The Thirty Years War furnished excellent pretexts for jousts between cats and rats, each camp changing its nationality depending on events, provided always that the people of Arras continued to be "rats." At the beginning of the hostilities they believed they were invincible: "When rats eat cats, / the French will take Arras," according to an old saying (Arras was then under Spanish rule). All the same, on 10 August 1640 Richelieu became master of the town; that is, the French cats took possession of the town held by the rats of Arras.[99] A contemporary engraving (see p. 30) shows a victorious cat wearing a conqueror's ruff, and the accompanying text reads: "When the French will take Arras, mice will eat cats. The French have taken Arras, and the mice haven't eaten one cat." The world upside down, in which the weak vanquish the strong, is decidedly only a dream.

An equally satirical engraving, dated 1641, depicts another episode in Arras's history (see p. 31). This time it has fallen to the cats to defend Spanish honor, no doubt because the rats of Arras had become French in the meantime. Before the town, the "Cats of Spain" are de-

Inside image:
ARRAS

Cartier cartier Messieurs les Ratz
Point de cartier Messieurs d'Arras.

L. Richerji.
G. Perelle fc

Gabriel Pérelle, Arras, 1641 engraving depicting the Spanish cats' defeat by the French rats in 1641, Arras, Archives du Pas-de-Calais.

feated by the rats' impetuous attack. In the foreground a cat brandishes a broken sword as the rats prepare to capture it.[100] The commentary says that "we see accomplished, Messieurs the inhabitants of Arras, / What your forefathers held up as prophecy": the rats' victory over the cats. This demonstrates that even the most fantastical and fanciful imagery never loses its roots in reality; and that, Spanish cats or no, the rats of Arras, like the city's valorous citizens who were flattered by the engraving, always played the hero's part.

It is for the painters to extract, if they wish, from the swarms of diverse, often contradictory meanings, what applies to the cat. Throughout the history of the arts, iconography has never been an iron yoke. In many cases, the cat is included solely for its esthetic appeal, its grace of movement and wealth of poses—because, in a word, it is itself a work of art. The chosen familiar of the artist's studio— mice gnaw canvas and cardboard just as they do grain—the cat will often compel the artist's attention and, in its discreet and mysterious feline way, will intermingle with the artist's palette.

Élisabeth Foucart-Walter

31

PER VN BACIO DATO
DA VNA BELLA E GRANDE SIGNORA
AD VN GATTO
SONETTO

Queſto ſcolpito in tela amabil Gatto,
Guſtò di Bella Dea bacio amoroſo,
E al Viuo poſcia fattone il Ritratto,
Si tien ben cuſtodito, e aſſai geloſo.

Affinchè poſſa appien ſerbarſi intatto
Qual Armellin, che uiue timoroſo,
E acciò preſo non ſia, ſen fugge ratto
A ſtare in Boſco, o in luogo piu naſcoſo.

Coſi Tu ancora, o Gatto auuenturato,
Serba intatta la Bocca, e puro il Core,
E à Colei penſa ſol, che ti ha baciato;

E fà che ſolo a Mè permetti Amore,
Che un Bacio ſcocchi e mi riprendi il dato
Bacio Amoroſo per temprar l'Ardore

Giovanni Reder, Portrait of Armellino with a sonnet by Bertazzi, Rome, Museo di Roma. Armellino was one of the first cats in history to be depicted alone in a portrait.

CATS AND PAINTERS

There have been "cat" painters and "non-cat" painters—that much is certain. But we know very little about the proclivities of early painters in this regard, since the artists themselves (unlike their peers, whether poets, writers, princes, ministers or kings) have told us nothing. Undoubtedly, some artists painted cats out of their love for them, and perhaps others omitted them from their works out of aversion. We are reduced to supposition. In contrast to the artists of our own time, who are usually more than delighted to discuss themselves, their lives and their cats (some even have had their pictures taken in the midst of their four-footed companions), painters in times past contented themselves with creating pictures, some of which included cats. Two particularly salient examples illustrate the contrast between our knowledge of the great figures of earlier times and what we know of those who painted them. On one hand, for instance, there was Richelieu and his great portraitist Philippe de Champaigne. All the world knows that the Cardinal doted on cats, but no one knows what feelings the somber Port-Royal painter entertained toward felines; he who in many of his most sacred scenes placed an aimiable tiger cat, so attentively rendered that it is clear the painter must often have observed it with understanding, tenderness and amusement (see pp. 108–109). Take, on the other hand, Louis XV and Francois Boucher: it is common knowledge that Louis "the Well-Beloved" was extremely fond of a beautiful white Angora, but nobody has ever wondered about the attachment Boucher, the painter of Rococo grace, must have felt for a comical cat with black eyebrows, which is found throughout the artist's *oeuvre* and could only have been his own (see pp. 136–137).

In leafing through Christabel Aberconway's charming and superabundant 1949 collection of cat lovers (from the fifteenth century B.C. up to the present), which is almost too seriously styled a "dictionary,"[101] we find that only one painter is listed. That is because artists express themselves less through confidences than through their works. It is up to us to retrace, through these paintings alone, the strange history of cats and those who have painted them.

CAT PAINTERS

In the 1850s, at the same time as some painters were specializing in flowers (in the so-called Fleur school of Lyons, for instance) or thoroughbreds or pedigree dogs (these last were a very English specialty), a growing number of painters began to choose cats as their subject—that is, they painted only cats throughout their careers. The cats they depicted were not necessarily pedigree. They were often rambunctious animals—cats or kittens enjoying frothy milk, playing with balls of yarn or bobbins of thread, or scaling the drawing-room piano. Many endearing genre scenes cropped up, most of which are too reminiscent of calendar illustrations to be taken seriously. For all that, we would be remiss not to include them, if only for sociological reasons. Such pictures represent the taste for quasi-photographic paintings—anecdotal in subject and almost exaggeratedly realistic—that spread across Europe at this time.

Contemptuously labeled "bourgeois," these pictures of cats have been carefully omitted from the histories of art, and their authors' names have almost all been ignored. But recently an extraordinary re-

Philippe Rousseau, The Unwelcome Guest, 1850, Paris, Ministry of Finance, depository of the Musée du Louvre.

newal of interest in these kinds of paintings has taken place, evidenced by the appearance of cat paintings of all genres and nationalities in French and (earlier) in London auctions.

In a recently published English dictionary of popular nineteenth-century genre paintings, an entire chapter is devoted to these pictures of cats and kittens, dogs and puppies (the latter are often shown with cats in order to create a *petite intrigue*).[102] The authors of the compilation counted no fewer than 182 painters who specialized in this area, three quarters of whom never painted anything else.

France's artists are well represented therein, and even the former museum of contemporary art, the famous Musée du Luxembourg, which has always been accused of favoring academic painting, had to bow to the craze for felines, acquiring, over a period of more than thirty-five years, two masterpieces of the genre. The first, *The Intruder* by Philippe Rousseau (1816–1887), was exhibited at the Salon of 1850–1851 (see p. 34).[103] The intruder is none other than a dog that unexpectedly interrupts the meal of a mother cat and her nursing kittens. Rousseau, who wished to be Chardin's successor, was not purely a cat specialist; Louis-Eugene Lambert (1825–1900), the creator of the second of the works at the Musée du Luxembourg—*The Cat Family*, exhibited at the 1887 Salon—painted nothing but works of this type all his life. This canvas, (housed at the Musée des Beaux-Arts in Tours since 1906) is a classic of its kind: a mother cat and her young, having climbed up on a table, play with the contents of a work basket while one of the kittens regards itself with astonishment in a mirror. Many other cat painters deserve mention, in addition to Lambert: Alphonse Brunel de Neuville (active 1878–1907), whose cats tip over an inkwell or inspect an insect that has fallen into their dish; Jules Leroy (1833–1865); Leon Charles Huber (1858–1928). The genre had many female specialists; for instance, Yvonne Laur (1879–?); Lucie Briard, who painted "musician" cats on a piano; and Jane d'Hazon (1874–?). In one of her canvases (exhibited at the 1899 Salon des Artistes français and evocatively titled *Maybug Flying! Young Cats*) some kittens and their mother, entangled in skeins of thread, attentively watch a flitting cockchafer. Two very surprising works by Gustave Bettinger also appeared in 1899.[104] In one, young and full-grown cats play with a mandolin and the pompom of a fan. Scorning to frolic in some bourgeois interior, they have slipped into the Holy of Holies, the royal apartments at Fontainebleau. Some have taken possession of the Cabinet of Theagène—one kitten has even hoisted itself up to the precious ivory casket that adorns one of the room's consoles—while others make themselves at home in the queen's chamber, a magnificent white Angora perches on one of Empress Josephine's armchairs, and two others sit on the Reisener chest of drawers.

Henriette Ronner-Knip, Cat with its Young, 1844, Amsterdam, Rijksmuseum.

Cat painters were perhaps less numerous in England, thanks to stiff competition from dogs in that nation of unrepentant hunters. But cats experienced a brilliant vogue in *fin-du-siècle* Germany: Julius Adam (1852–1913) of Munich, the equivalent of the French Louis-Eugene Lambert, painted unruly young cats that owe nothing to their French cousins; so did Johannes Siegwald Dahl (1827–1902), Arthur Heyer (1872–1931) and Hermine Biedermann-Arendts (1855)?).

Belgium, with Charles van den Eycken (1859–1923), is also on the list, but is clearly outdistanced by the neighboring Netherlands, which can boast of Cornelis Raaphorst (1875–1954) and, above all, Henriette Ronner-Knip (1821–1909). The latter, a Rosa Bonheur of felines, is certainly the best known. Her masterpiece remains the 1844 painting (see p. 35) of a superb ruddy cat sitting on a sumptuous cushion with its tabby and white youngsters in the embrasure of a rustic window framed with ivy and flowers, all rendered in the manner of one of the great masters of the Dutch Golden Age such as Dou or Van Ostade.

In fact, all of these painters, as specialized and commercial as they may have been, shared a craft that was at once precise, gentle and ingenious—perfectly suited to the depiction of a cat's soft fur, clear, deep gaze and sinuous grace. What more can we say, without reproaching these artists for painting too well, from the present point of view—for possessing too perfect, too virtuosic a technique; in brief, for having depicted the cat as we see it rather than as the artist might have recreated it.

Gottfried Mind, the "Raphael of cats," Portrait of two cats.

One Swiss cat painter has carved out a special niche. This is Gottfried Mind (1768–1814). Working on the periphery of all the trends and also older than the preceding artists, he was nicknamed the "Raphael of cats" and was well known for his almost unhealthy worship of the feline race. Champfleury devotes an entire chapter to Mind in his book *Les Chats*,[105] and Mind is, notably, the sole painter listed in Aberconway's astonishing dictionary of cat lovers. When he wasn't drawing or painting cats, he was sculpting them out of chestnuts. He painted bears as a sideline, but nothing else. In 1809, during a rabies epidemic in Bern, more than 800 cats had to be destroyed. Mind, the story goes, succeeded in spiriting his *"bien-aimée"* Minette away, but he was nonetheless traumatized by the event, and never got over it.

*Léonard Foujita, The Artist and His Cat, 1928,
Centre Georges-Pompidou, Musée national d'Art moderne.*

Upon Mind's death, a wag amused himself by parodying Catullus's verses on the death of a sparrow: *Lugete, o feles, ursique lugete, / Mortuus est vobis amicus* (Cry, oh cats; weep, bears: Your great friend is dead). The cats in Mind's sketches, watercolors or paintings are easily recognized: rather naive in style, they often wear a disturbing smile, and their almost human gaze betrays something of their beloved creator's strange personality (see p. 35). Mind's works very quickly garnered success among both art lovers and cat lovers. Frédéric Villot, a friend of Delacroix and curator of paintings at the Louvre during the Second Empire (his claim to fame lies in his compilation of the museum's catalogues), had in his collection some of Mind's cats, which he permitted Champfleury to reproduce.

Some artists, without specializing in cats, nevertheless excelled at portraying them. The Swiss artist Théophile Alexandre Steinlen (1859–1923), that valorous adopted citizen of the Butte Montmartre, is certainly the artist to whom the feline tribe most owes its artistic celebrity. Steinlen's numerous drawings and humorous illustrations demonstrate a perfect knowledge of cats' gestures and actions that is not without a certain cruel irony. This quality is abundantly evident in *The Horrible End of a Goldfish*—one of the most pointed of his illustrations to appear in the review *Le Chat noir* (3 May 1884)—in which we witness a merciless struggle between a cat and fish. No less famous are his posters paying homage to cats: *Pure, Sterilized Milk From the Vingeanne* (1894), in which we see a little girl gulping down a bowl of milk under the envious gaze of three cats; or the poster created in 1896 at the request of Rodolphe de Salis for the Chat noir cabaret in Paris. But in addition to his decorative and graphic works, Steinlen created great paintings of cats (see p. 41). The same realistic fervor animates his pictures of strikers and tramps and his painting of cats eating offal (Musée de Vernon). His handsome animals, most often tabby or black, drowse, their almond eyes half closed (Geneva, Musée du Petit Palais; Paris, Musée d'Orsay)—that is, if they are not being held upright on their hind legs by a girl little bigger than they, but possessed of an audacious and charming familiarity (Geneva, Musée du Petit Palais). At the opposite extreme from the Franco-Swiss Steinlen is the Japanese artist Léonard Foujita (1886–1968). The cat shown on his shoulder in his countless self-portraits (see p. 36), is a virtual confidant. Often it fixes us with a gaze as insistent as the painter's. To a certain degree, the suppleness of cats' poses is well suited to the innate sense of line in Far Eastern calligraphy, which Fujita plainly possessed: witness his many lithographs of cats and, above all, an unbelievable 1940 painting (Tokyo, National Museum), an unbridled roundelay of cats in wildly diverse poses. It forms a kind of challenge *à la japonaise*, a somewhat stylized, slightly terrifying response to the paintings of Jan Fyt (see p. 105).

Painters With or Without Cats

Few artists find favor in Champfleury's *Les Chats* (published in 1868–1869)—a work that is, it must be said, rather banal and conventional for a critic who considered himself avant-garde in all things. *Les Chats* praises the Egyptian and Far Eastern "artists" almost too much, while it accuses our early painters of "having found their models in toy stores and taxidermists' shops." Champfleury adds that the cat in Venius's *Otto Venius Painting, Surrounded by His Family* (see pp. 82–83) "appears to have been stuffed with bran." This curious and disappointing observation leads one to wonder about Champfleury's artistic sensibility and the limits of a critic whose criteria were too narrowly "realistic" and a bit too submissive to the tastes of the times (the end of the Second Empire).

Champfleury does not mention Manet among his contemporaries, although he took the famous engraving after the artist's sketch, entitled *The Cats' Rendezvous*, to illustrate his book, and enlarged the same for a publicity poster. And according to Champfleury, Eugène Delacroix (1798–1863) was, on account of his "feverish and nervous" nature, the artist best predisposed to portray cats. Unfortunately, the critic states, he contented himself with merely drawing them; in his paintings, they are transformed into tigers. Doubtless this strange metamorphosis took place in the critic's mind alone. It is well known that Delacroix, in the company of Barye (1795–1875), would often draw the big cats at Paris's Jardins des Plantes alive as well as under dissection, in order to study their anatomy.[107]

In fact, at least one painter can be accused of having changed a cat into a giant beast of prey. This artist was Gustave Moreau (1826–1898), who, while staying at Étampes with his friend Narcisse Berchère, the Oriental landscape painter, amused himself by drawing the latter's cat, named Qui-Qui. In a drawing that shows a terrifying large feline, we read, in the artist's hand, the annotation, "Étampes. Qui-Qui transformed into a panther" (see p. 37). The sleight-of-hand has taken place, and an inoffensive little domestic pet has thus become, through the artist's magic pencil, a savage panther.

Champfleury lauds the talents of Philibert Rouvière (1809–1865), who had interrupted his career as a painter to become an actor (Manet portrayed him as Hamlet). According to the critic, Rouvière's feline nature led him to excel at depicting cats. Champfleury's argument is rather slender, and to a certain extent one understands why. Many painters have indeed drawn cats marvelously, but have shied away from including them in their paintings. The reason is simple: in a first draft, an artist may enjoy the virtuosic exercise of sketching a cat from life, but he may not find it necessary to include the animal in the painting that follows. The Neo-Classical work of François-André Vincent (1746–1816) is instructive in this regard. Absolutely no cats are evident in his canvases of scenes from ancient Rome or French history, but an extraordinary sheet of paper, signed and dated Rome, 1772, is crammed with life studies of cats (see p. 37). The young artist, then a pensioner at the Académie de France, also executed caricatures of his friends, exhibiting a graphic skill that is unequaled save in his pictures of cats rolled into sleeping balls or washing themselves.

In Rome several artists amused themselves by slipping cats into some of their first drafts. For example, a caricature engraving (after a drawing by Jean-Baptiste Stouf) of the silhouettes of several artists in Rome in about 1770, one of whom is named Julien (Julien de Parme or Simon Julien?), includes a cat. "Ingrisme" lent itself no more to the anecdotal inclusion of cats than did Neo-Classicism. Nonetheless, Ingres loved cats, and in Jean Alaux's 1818 painting of Ingres' studio on Rome's Via Gregoriana we see a little white cat curled up not far from the artist, who holds his sacrosanct violin (Montauban, Musée Ingres). Besides, Ingres himself did a rapid pen-sketch of a cat, *Madame Ingres's Cat in Her Arms* (Montauban, Musée Ingres). But it is to one of his students, Amaury-Duval (1808–1885), that we owe one of the most unexpected cats of Ingrisme. Amaury-Duval, steeped in the same climate of study and leisure that Vincent enjoyed nearly forty years earlier, drew several cats in a booklet of sketches inspired by Italian life (see p. 38). In one particularly memorable street-corner scene, a colossal Roman butcher or cook stalks a small cat that hides

Gustave Moreau, Qui-Qui transformed into a panther, Paris, Musée Gustave Moreau.

François-André Vincent, Study of a Cat (detail), 1772, Paris, Institut néerlandais, Fondation Custodia.

Amaury-Duval, *Scene from Roman Life*,
Autun, Musée Rodin.

behind a milestone; the cat is evoked with a few pencil strokes, in an allusive, ironic style that bears little resemblance to the serious, linear craft favored by the decorator of the churches of Saint-Merry and Saint-Germain-l'Auxerrois in Paris.

There are many other unsuspected cat sketchers who did not permit felines to appear in their *"grands peintures."* Prix de Rome winner Joseph Barthélemy le Bouteux (1744–?) displays a genuine talent for depicting animals in a red chalk drawing of a sleeping cat (Besançon, Musée des Beaux-Arts). A drawing of a cat (see p. 39) by the landscape painter Hendrik Voogd (1768–1839), active in Italy, is one of the most impressive in the history of art (Dresden, Staatliche Kunstsammlungen). Majestic and distant, the animal seems to give itself airs; its fur, rendered with an incomparable tactile density, irresistibly recalls a bovine head that Voogd also executed (Quimper, Musée des Beaux-Arts). No less astounding are the four studies of cats, head to tail, discovered on the back of a drawing by the Danish artist Christen Købke (1810–1848). Here the animal is more summarily treated, as if the artist were primarily interested in capturing its outline, drawn from nature (Paris, Institut néerlandais, Fondation Custodia).

This leads us to the studies executed in paint, a genre unto itself at which Peter Boel, Jan Fyt and François Desportes excelled (see p. 118, p. 105, p. 128). In their studies they continued to depict cats savagely yowling, leaping and clawing—unforgettable, virtuosic images without which the history of cats in painting could not have been written. A painter—perhaps the Dutch artist Nicolaes Berchem (1620–1683)—executed, on the back of a letter, three pictures in oil of a black-and-white cat in mid-leap.[107] If we cannot call these studies great paintings, let us at least acknowledge them as the brilliant achievements of painters who wished to capture on canvas the instant of a cat's pounce, the split-second of a paw-blow. Does not the cat, with its swift, supple movements, embody the very idea of motion? It is easy to understand why Etienne-Jules Marey chose to use cats in his celebrated photographic experiments of 1894.

Portraits of Cats

It is said that *portrait* implies a model with a specific identity, but it is difficult to talk about portraits from truly ancient times, when there were no models as we understand them. In early art, cats are to be found everywhere, but specific cats are found nowhere. The depiction of cats as individuals began relatively late, much later than it did with other animals. The cat, in contrast to the dog or the horse, was not considered a noble or pedigree animal, and we search in vain for an Italian palace comparable to the Palazzo del Té in Mantua, where, instead of the most beautiful horses in the Gonzaga stables, a prince's remarkable cats were painted. As cats did not accompany their masters in the hunt, they were not entitled to the same honors as were the dogs in the kennels of Louis XIV and Louis XV, who had Desportes and Oudry paint portraits of their hounds, complete with names (Ponne, Bonne, Nonne, Pompée, Florissant, Polydore . . .). The handful of rare and famous cats cited herein have, with one Italian exception, remained anonymous and cannot ultimately be defined save in relation to their masters. Not until our own century have cats entered the scene under their own names: Suzanne Valadon's Raminou (see p. 205) has become a very important figure in the history of cat portraits. So have Vollard's Lulu, Cecilia Beaux's Sita (see p. 189), Albert Gleizes's Riquet (drawing in the Fondation nationale des Arts graphiques et plastiques, Paris), or Tiger, painted by Gwen John

(1876–1939), who so often depicted herself with a cat on her lap.

One of the finest and doubtless oldest portrayals of a cat is extant in the 1657 engraving entitled *Large Cat* by the Dutch artist Cornelis Visscher (ca. 1619–1662). In this veritable *tour de force* crouches a cat, and behind it a mouse (see p. 39). Even if one can discern a certain complicity between the artist and his model—which could only be his own cat—it would obviously be inappropriate to label this engraving a "portrait." Is this not also the case in a painting that Bachelier exhibited at the 1761 Salon (see p. 138), which is the first cat to be individualized in such a way? The fact that the cat is shown with a bird, and that originally the canvas had a painting of a dog as a pendant, suggests a truly "encyclopedic" painstakingness—perhaps in response to the eminent naturalist George-Louis de Buffon, who hated cats. The cat is a lovely animal, one of the precious white Angoras reputedly introduced into France by Rubens' correspondant, the erudite ama-

Hendrik Voogd, Study of a Cat's Head (detail), Dresden, Staatliche Kunstsammlungen.

teur Nicolas-Claude de Peiresc (1580–1637). Indeed, Bachelier's depiction may arise more out of a naturalist's curiosity than a cat lover's admiring observation.

A cat's personality depends, in fact, on that of its master. From robust, even extravagant personalities have come celebrated cats recognized as worthy of portraits in their own right. Let us quickly add that these feline celebrities are extremely rare. One of the first belonged to Sir Henry Wyatt (1460–1537), a notable figure at the English court, who was portrayed by Holbein the Younger (1497/1498–1543) (Paris, Musée du Louvre). During the reign of Richard III, Wyatt was locked up in the grimmest royal prison for his support of the Lancastrian cause. He would have starved or frozen to death without the almost miraculous intervention of his cat, which brought him pigeons (already cooked, according to some biographers) and huddled on his chest to warm him.[108] Such fidelity surely merited a portrait, and one was indeed painted quite a bit later, perhaps only in the eighteenth century. In this naive but very moving work, the painter (of modest talent) transferred Holbein's portrait to a prison milieu and depicted the English dignitary face to face with his feline savior.

Another personality, this time Parisian, later enlivened the chronicles of cats. This was one Mlle. Dupuy, a celebrated mid-seventeenth-century harpist. She attributed to her pet "the excellence which she had attained. It listened attentively every time she practiced her harp, and displayed different degrees of interest and affection in the same measure as her execution possessed more or less precision and harmony."[109] That, at least, is how Moncrif, author of the famous

Cornelis Visscher, Large Cat, engraving, 1657, Paris, Institut néerlandais, Fondation Custodia.

Engraving after Charles-Antoine Coypel, illustrating Moncrif's Histoire des Chats, 1727.

History of Cats (published in Paris in 1727), described this astonishing maestro's qualities. Also according to Moncrif, Mlle. Dupuy, who died on 7 October 1677, had her will made in favor of the animal, in recognition of its contributions. There is some basis to the story: Mlle. Dupuy's will indeed mentions her two cats, recommending that they be well fed "with bread, broth and meat soup" and that "30 sous a month be reserved for them." The affair undoubtedly caused a stir at the time, and as of about 1680 an engraving of Mlle. Dupuy's cat was published as the counterpart to the depiction of a dog owned by the king of Sweden; Charles-Antoine Coypel (1694–1752), who was commissioned to illustrate Moncrif's book, did a drawing, engraved by the Comte de Caylus, of the lady dictating her will. Coypel has depicted the cat ensconced on its beloved mistress's bed, but it is above all the two astounded notaries, stupefied at such a last testament, who rightly command our attention.

Moncrif also reports that a Mme. de Lesdiguières (1655–1716) raised for her cat a tombstone crowned with a posthumous "portrait" of the deceased in full relief. The epitaph read: "Here lies a pretty cat: its mistress, who never loved anyone, / loved it madly; / Why bother to say so? Everyone can see it." Again, the drawing for Caylus' engraving was by Coypel; undoubtedly an ironic sketch, it admittedly reveals nothing of the great cat painter's talent (see p. 40).

A true portrait (see p. 32) is the painting of Armellino, a cat that belonged to an eighteenth-century Roman poetess, Alessandra Forteguerra, born Rospigliosi.[110] The author of this surprising figure is the painter Giovanni Reder (1693–?), who was born into an artistic family that specialized in horses. He sets the cat, its neck adorned with an elegant belled collar, on a sumptuous cushion; on the heavy fringed curtain that frames the cat hangs a sonnet by the poet Abbott Sperandio Bertazzi, singing the praises of this unexpected model.

Finally, there remains a certain white cat, whose identity one would love to know, since it would perhaps lead us to those of its master and creator. It is the *White Cat* (see p. 6) at the Ny Carlsberg Glyptotek in Copenhagen; its attribution to Gericault is sometimes contested (rightly?). Whatever it is, this marvelously well painted animal deserves a place, as an unidentified model, in the anthology of cats portrayed on their own merits. In this truly astonishing painting, the artist, has not focused much on the cat's head, a shame, when one considers the sharpness of the feline gaze. Instead, he has concentrated on its white fur, which is rendered both silky and sculptural through the workings of the pictorial material and the play of brilliant lights against profound darks.

In considering all of these cats, whether they pose as the chosen subject or crouch forgotten in a corner of the canvas, are we not struck by something strange? Some of these cats bear a curious resemblance to the women and men at their sides. Jan Steen's sickly cat grimaces in the same way as the rumpled boy who teases it; Jordaens's huge tomcat narrows its eyes just like the king who lifts cup to lips; Boilly's cream-furred Angora peers about with eyes as round as those of its young mistress. And does not Millet's anxious, sad gutter stray wear on its face all the heavy rusticity of the peasants' life?

These artists did not intend—as did Charles Le Brun, or, two centuries later, Grandville—to play the fascinating and disturbing game of "physiognomy," deliberately giving men the animals' characteristics, or vice-versa. Without meaning to, they allowed the cat to assume a place in their most intimate repertoire. It is yet one more proof that the cat was made for the mysterious, silent language that is painting.

Élisabeth Foucart-Walter and Pierre Rosenberg

Théophile Alexandre Steinlen, Cat on an Armchair,
Paris, Musée d'Orsay.

NOTES

1. Books about cats abound; serious studies of their iconography are rare. H. van de Waal, *Iconclass, Bibliography*, 2–3 (Amsterdam, 1973), p. 287, no. 34 B 12; the article "Cat" indicates the principle bibliographic references on the subject. One is surprised to learn the *Lexikon der christlichen Ikonographie* (Rome, Fribourg-en-Brisgau, Basel, Vienna, 8 vols., 1968–1976), extensive in other respects, says nothing about cats.

2. Erwin Panofsky, *Albrecht Durer* (Princeton, 1948), vol. I, pp. 84–87, vol. II, p. 21, no. 108.

3. Cf. M. Oldfield Howey, *The Cat in the Mysteries of Religion and Magic* (republished in four printings; London, ca. 1930–1931; Philadelphia, 1932; New York, ca. 1955–1956; Rutland, U.S.A., and Tokyo, 1981), chap. VIII, "Christ and the Cat," pp. 62–65. The author, without any hesitation, recounts the farfetched story of the female cat giving birth in the creche, which he borrows in toto from a work by G. J. Ouseley (cf. following note). Other "historians" take up this tale in their turn: for example, Patricia Dale-Green, *Cult of the Cat* (London, Melbourne, Toronto, 1963), p. 45; and George Ferguson, *Signs and Symbols in Christian Art* (Oxford and New York), s.d., p. 8, who believes the sign of the cross can be seen on the backs of certain cats (doubtless tabbies) present in religious scenes.

4. *The Gospel of the Holy Twelve, written down and pub. by the late Rev. G. J. Ouseley* (London, new edition, 1923), cited by M. Oldfield Howey, *op. cit.*, p. 64.

5. Rev. G. J. Ouseley, cited by M. Oldfield Howey, *op. cit.*, pp. 64–65.

6. Conference of 7 January 1668, see Henry Jouin, *Conférences de l'Académie royale de Peinture et de Sculpture* (Paris, 1883), pp. 64–65. The Champaigne discussed at this conference surely could only be Philippe de Champaigne, not his nephew Jean-Baptiste as Jacques Thuillier supposed (*Colloque Poussin*, vol. II, p. 143, note 4) on the basis of a first-draft manuscript account of the conference, in which the name Champaigne le Jeune appears. In the definitive version intended for publication, Guillet de Saint-Georges carefully changed "le jeune" to "l'aisné."

7. On the meaning of the cat in the Annunciation, see Mrs. Jameson, *Legends of the Madonna* (London, new edition, 1899), p. 178, who calls the inclusion of such cats intolerable.

8. One of these Annunciations with cats is at the Thyssen Collection in Lugano-Castagnola; in 1966 the other was in the Wetzlar Collection in Amsterdam.

9. Herbert Friedmann, *The Symbolic Goldfinch, its History and Significance in European Devotional Art*, Bollingen Series VII (Washington, D.C.: Pantheon Books, 1946). Also Mrs. Jameson, *op. cit.*, pp. xlvii–xlviii, 71–72.

10. The Louvre has a modest copy; another of much better quality was in the holdings of New York's Metropolitan Museum of Art, but was sold in 1973.

11. Paul Michel, *Tiere als Symbol und Ornament. Möglichkeiten und Grenzen der ikonographischen Deutung, gezeigt am Beispiel des zürcher Grossmünsterkreuzgangs* (Weisbaden), p. 124.

12. Bernard Dorival, "Philippe de Champaigne et les *Hiéroglyphiques* de Pierus," *Revue de l'Art* (1971), no. 11, pp. 34–35; and *Philippe de Champaigne 1602–1674: La vie, l'oeuvre et le catalogue raisonné de l'oeuvre* (1976), vol. II, p. 50, no. 78. Cesare Ripa, in his description of the sixth hour ("Hora Sesta"), takes the cat to be a "hieroglyphe" of the moon (*Iconologia*, 1611, reprint 1976, pp. 228–29, repr.

13. On the theme of Emmaus, see Lucien Rudrauf, *Le Repas d'Emmaüs: Etude d'un thème plastique et de ses variations en peinture et sculpture* (Paris, 1955–1956), 2 vols. In this work, in which about 273 examples of the Supper at Emmaus are reproduced, we find seventeen cats—ten shown with dogs, and seven by themselves. The artists whose depictions of the Supper at Emmaus contain cats are fairly evenly divided among the Italians (Marziale, Pontormo—a unique case with *two* cats, Tintoretto, Bassano, Moretto, Raphael, Faccini . . .) and the Northern artists (Jordaens, Goltzius, Floris, Heemskerk . . .). The motif's rarity in France is noteworthy (Callot and Champaigne). Chronologically speaking, it is markedly absent from works of the Middle Ages and the modern era.

14. Marcel Uzé, *Le Chat dans la nature, dans l'histoire et dans l'art* (Paris, 1951), p. 16.

15. Monseigneur X. Barbier de Montault, *Traité d'iconographie chrétienne* (Paris, 1890; new edition, 1900), vol. II, p. 308. Louis Réau, *Iconographie de l'Art chrétien*, vol. III, *Iconographie des saints. I.* (Paris, 1958), p. 254: "Saint Cadoc"; according to the attributes listed by Réau (*op. cit.*, *Iconographie des saints. III.*, 1959, p. 105), Cadoc was the only saint with a cat. See also Gerd Heinz-Mohr, *Lexikon der Symbole: Bilder und Zeichen der christlichen Kunst* (Eugen Diederichs Verlag, 1971), p. 154.

16. Wood engraving, sparingly colored by *pochoir*, published "A Rennes, chez Pierret fils, Impr. Oberthur. 1863."

17. Monseigneur X. Barbier de Montault, *op. cit.*, vol. II, p. 439.

18. Ibid., vol. I, p. 169; vol. II, p. 341.

19. Smith Thompson, *Motif-Index of Folk Literature* (Copenhagen), 10 vols., vol. I (1955), p. 251.

20. A. P. de Mirimonde, *Sainte Cécile, Métamorphoses d'un thème musical* (Geneva, 1974), p. 121, fig. 96: engraving published in 1782 by Humphrey, New Bond Street, London.

21. See the exhibition catalogue *Romanische Kunst in Oesterreich* (Krems an der Donau, 1964), pp. 87–93. On the subject of cats and mice, see H. van de Waal, *op. cit.*, pp. 287–88, no. 34 B 12, 1.

22. The most famous "Murr" cat is in the *Contes* of Hoffmann. It inspired a painting by Charles Renoux (Salon of 1835, no. 1820); another by Vicomte Ludovic-Napoléon Lepic (1870; New York, Shepherd Gallery, 1987); finally, King Don Fernando of Portugal, an amateur artist, did an engraving of the subject (see Alfred Busquet, "Les Dessins et les Eaux-Fortes de roi Don Fernando," *Gazette des Beaux-Arts* 5, 1 February 1860, pp. 155–58, repr.).

23. Rösli and Edgar Schumacher, *Das Katzenbuch: Ein Brevier* (Zurich, 1939), p. 62, repr.

24. See the exhibition catalogue *Ketters en papen onder Filips II* (Utrecht, Rijksmuseum Het Catharijneconvent, 1986), pp. 174–75, repr. fig. 109.

25. *Corréspondance inédite de l'abbé Ferdinand Galiani, conseiller du roi, pendant les années 1765 à 1783* (Paris, 1818), vol. I, p. 191: letter of 22 December 1770, written in Naples.

26. Guy de Tervarent, *Attributs et Symboles dans l'art profane, 1450–1600: Dictionnaire d'un langage perdu* (Geneva, 1958), vol. I, p. 90. Margaret Armbrust Seibert, "A Political and a Pictorial Tradition Used in Gustave Courbet's *Real Allegory*," *Art Bulletin*, June 1983, pp. 311–16 (in discussing the cat in *The Artist's Studio*, the author uncovers its various allegorical meanings).

27. Arthur Henkel and Albrecht Schöne, *Emblemata: Handbuch zur Sinnbildkunst des XVI. und XVII. Jahrhunderts, Sonderausgabe* (Stuttgart, 1978), col. 1348, repr. from Nicolaus Taurellus, *Emblemata . . .* (Nuremburg, 1602), no. 8.

28. Cesare Ripa, *Iconologia* (Padua, 1611; Garland reprint, New York and London, 1976), pp. 312–13.

29. Cited after the French translation of 1636, illustrated with medallions engraved by Jacques de Brie, often consulted by French artists. In his original text, Ripa mentions two other peoples that used cats in their war ensignia: the Iranian Alans and the Germanic Suebi. Some say that because the cat symbolized Liberty several printers (including Sessa of Venice) adopted it as their emblem in the sixteenth century.

30. A. Henkel and A. Schöne, *op. cit.*, col. 588, from Joachim Camerarius, *Symbolorum et emblematum ex animalibus quadrupedibus . . .* (Nuremberg, 1595), no. 78.

31. Jose Maria de Azcárate, "La alegoria en *Las Hilanderas*," *Varia Velazqueña* (Madrid, 1960), vol. I, pp. 344–51.

32. This plaster medallion is so integral a part of the decor of the royal apartments at Compiègne (along with the *trompe-l'oeil* door carving by the painter Sauvage, which imitates the bas-relief) that we decided to include it in this text, which in principle deals only with cats in the graphic arts.

33. M. A. Seibert, *op. cit.*, pp. 315–16. See also Théophile Gautier, "Concours pour la Figure de la République," *La Presse*, 21 May 1848, cited by Marie-Claude Chaudonneret, *La Figure de la République: Le Concours de 1848* (Paris, 1987), p. 144 and Champfleury, *Les Chats* (Paris, 1869), third ed., pp. 49–50. More farcically still, the poet Guyot-Desherbiers, who took an active part in the French Revolution, saw this "revolutionary" cat as a reincarnation of the cat Haret, worshiped by the Gauls (see P. Mégnin, *Notre ami le chat*, Paris, p. 111).

34. G. de Tervarent, *op. cit.*, p. 90.

35. *Op. cit.*, 1611, pp. 101–102 ("Contrasto"), p. 253 ("Inimicitia").

36. *Op. cit.*, 1611, p. 419 ("Persuasione").

37. A lost painting, the photograph of which is part of the papers of A. P. de Mirimonde, bequeathed to the Louvre in 1985.

38. See the exhibition catalogue *L'Allégorie dans la peinture, la représentation de la Charité au XVIIe siècle* (Caen, Musée des Beaux-Arts), no. 5, repr. (discussion by Alain Tapié); and *Le Livre des peintres de Carel van Mander . . .*, translated by Hymans (1885), vol. II, p. 252.

39. A. Henkel and A. Schöne, *op. cit.* Dr. F. A. Stoett, *Nederlandsche Spreekwoorden, Spreekwijzen, Uitdrukkingen en Gezegden*, fourth ed., Pt. 1 (Zutphen, 1943), pp. 428–35.

40. R. and E. Schumacher, *op. cit.*, p. 61, repr.

41. Juliette Raabe, *Bibliothèque illustrée du chat*, vol. II, ed. de la Courtille, p. 99, repr.

42. Jacob Cats, *Spiegel van den ouden ende nieuwen tijd* (The Hague, 1632). The edition used here is *Alle de Wercken van de Heere Jacob Cats* (Amsterdam, 1712).

43. Ibid., 1712, p. 523.

44. Ibid., p. 541.

45. Ibid., p. 528.

46. Ibid., p. 530.

47. J. Raabe, *op. cit.*, vol. I, p. 128, repr.

48. J. Cats, 1712, p. 638.

49. A. Henkel and A. Schöne, *op. cit.*, col. 589, repr. from Florentinus Schoonhovius, *Emblemata . . .* (Gouda, 1618).

50. The principle La Fontaine fables that involve a cat are: *La Chatte métamorphosée en femme; L'Aigle, la Laie et la Chatte; Le Chat et le Vieux Rat; Le Coche, le Chat et le Souriceau; Le Chat et le Rat; Le Chat, la Belette et le Petit Lapin; Le Rat et l'Éléphant; Le Chat et le Renard; Le Singe et le Chat; Le Chat et les Deux Moineaux; Le Vieux Chat et la Jeune Souris; La Quer-*

elle des chiens et des chats, et celle des chats et des souris; La Ligue des rats. Of La Fontaine's illustrators—too numerous to name—we mention one of the most famous: Jean-Baptiste Oudry (see Hal Opperman, exhibition catalogue *J. B. Oudry 1686–1755* (Paris, Grand Palais, 1982–1983), pp. 157–64). Oudry is also the author of a canvas on the fable of the cat and the monkey, part of a group painted in 1720 on the subject of La Fontaine's fables (Sotheby's auction, Monte Carlo, 20 June 1987, no. 388).

51. A. Henkel and A. Schöne, *op. cit.*, col. 586–87, repr. from Dionysius Lebeus-Batillius, *Dionysii Lebei-Batillii . . . emblemata* (Frankfurt am Main, 1596), no. 39.

52. J. Cats, *op. cit.*, p. 509.

53. Ibid., p. 619. See also Annelies Plokker, *Adriaen Pietersz. van de Venne (1589–1662). De grisailles met spreukbanden* (Louvain, Amersfoort, 1984), pp. 140–41, no. 51, repr.

54. A. Henkel and A. Schöne, *op. cit.*, col. 586, repr. from Joannes Sambucus, *Emblemata . . .* (Antwerp, 1566), p. 125.

55. J. Raabe, *op. cit.*, vol. I, pp. 58–59: engraving by Gerhart Altzenbach, editor and perhaps also engraver, active in Cologne (and possibly Strasbourg) in the seventeenth century.

56. A. Henkel and A. Schöne, *op. cit.*, col. 587, from Nicolaus Taurellus, *op. cit.*, H.

57. Ibid., col. 592, repr. from J. Cats, *Proteus ofte Minne-beelden Verandert In Sinne-beelden* (Rotterdam, 1627), 12, 1.

58. Ibid., col. 593–94, repr. from J. Cats, *op. cit.*, note above, 18, 1.

59. Ibid., col. 591, repr. from Daniel Heinsius, *Het Ambacht Van Cupido . . .* (Leyden, 1615), no. 44.

60. See the exhibition catalogue *Von Frans Hals bis Vermeer, Meisterwerke Holländischer Genremalerie* (Berlin, Gemäldegalerie, 1984), no. 125, pp. 340–42, repr.

61. See the exhibition catalogue *Tot Lering en Vermaak* (Amsterdam, Rijksmuseum, 1976), no. 76, pp. 284–87, repr.

62. For instance, *The Dead Mouse* by P. Van Slingeland at the Smidt van Gelder Museum in Antwerp.

63. Another version of the Karlsruhe painting is at the Hermitage in Leningrad.

64. See the exhibition catalogue *Die Sprache der Bilder* (Brunswick, Herzog Anton Ulrich-Museum, 1978), no. 23, pp. 116–19, repr.

65. A. Henkel and A. Schöne, *op. cit.*, col. 588–89, repr. from Jacobus Bruck, *Emblemata politica*, 1618, no. 50.

66. Ibid., col. 588, repr. from N. Taurellus, *op. cit.*, G 4.

67. The Musée du Berry at Bourges has a curious and naive "portrait" (Flemish or Dutch) of a cat and a dog side by side in perfect harmony. An indecipherable text doubtless expounds the moral of this unaccustomed image.

68. Exhibition catalogue *Mari et Femme dans la France rurale traditionelle* (Paris, Musée des Arts et Traditions populaires, 1973), no. 179, repr. on the cover.

69. The painting's owner had it completed in the upper floor of his house to fit the chimney exactly.

70. Eighteenth-century French school (attributed first to Fragonard, then to the German school); its pendant is another canvas of a monkey, a dog, and a child near a goldfish bowl. The two paintings have been deposited by the Louvre with the Mobilier national.

71. Frédérick Tristan, *Le Monde à l'envers* (Paris, 1980).

72. The evocation of the world upside down in Heinrich and Margarethe Schmidt, *Die Vergessene Bildersprache Kunst: Ein Führer um Verständnis der Tier-. Engel, und Mariensymbolik* (Munich, 1981), pp. 122–23.

73. A. Henkel and A. Schöne, *op. cit.*, col. 595, from Hadrianus Junius, *Emblemata . . .* (Antwerp, 1565), no. 4.

74. Ibid., col. 595, from J. Camerarius, *op. cit.*, no. 89.

75. Sold at Christie's auction, London, 5 July 1985, no. 93, color repr.

76. Jean Adhémar, *Imagerie populaire française* (Milan, 1968), no. 38: engraving published in Paris "chez la veuve Montcornet, rue St-Jacques vis-à-vis St-Yves," ca. 1640 (Paris, Bibliothèque nationale, Cabinet des estampes).

77. For the different depictions of cats in the world upside down, see F. Tristan, *op. cit.*, figs. 98, 109, 113, 114, 116, 120, 122, 143, 160, 163, 165, 166 (among others).

78. Location unknown, reference from the "Cat" dossier at the Warburg Institute in London.

79. Luc Benoist, *Catalogue du Musée des Beaux-Arts de Nantes*, p. 107, no. 294. See also two other works attributed to Frangipani—one at the Musée des Beaux-Arts in Angers—containing rather equivocal implications. They depict people singing and laughing, along with cats that are much more anecdotal in nature. See in this regard P. Bautier, "Un peintre italien de XVIe siècle influencé par nos maitres drôles," *Revue belge d'archéologie et d'histoire d'art*, 1958, 1–4,

pp. 63–67, repr.

80. Maria Adelaide Baroncelli, *Faustino Bocchi ed Enri Albrici, pittori di Bambocciate* (Brescia, 1965).

81. The Louvre owns a contemporaneous copy.

82. Ulrich Chr. Haldi, "Le Corps de garde de singes," *Galerie Stuker Blätter* (Bern, April 1982) no. 7, pp. 8–9.

83. *Cats Led Before a Military Tribunal of Monkeys*, the pendant to *The Guard Corps of Monkeys* (which has no cats), both at the Louvre.

84. Numerous versions of this composition exist.

85. A. P. de Mirimonde, "Les Concerts parodiques chez les maîtres du Nord," *Gazette des Beaux-Arts*, November 1964, pp. 253–84, particularly pp. 258, 261–263.

86. J. Raabe, *op. cit.*, vol. I, p. 69, repr., engraving by Françoise Ragot; "fecit et excud. à Paris, rue S. Jacques à Lelephan."

87. F. Tristan, *op. cit.*, p. 62, fig. 56, seventeenth-century satiric French engraving.

88. A. P. de Mirimonde, *op. cit.*, p. 258, fig. 10; see also Champfleury, *op. cit.*, pp. 38–39, and P. Mégnin, *op. cit.*, p. 55.

89. Ibid., p. 263, repr. fig. 14, 15.

90. See in this respect the work of M. Oldfield Howey, *op. cit.*, who links the cat's symbolism too tightly to a world of demonic superstitions and occult mysteries.

91. Hans Baldung Grien often associated cats with sorceresses—for instance, in an important drawing at the Albertina in Vienna; see the exhibition catalogue *Les Sorcières* (Paris, Bibliothèque nationale, 1973), no. 67, repr., in which one finds other witches with cats.

92. Fausta Franchini Guelfi, *Alessandro Magnasco* (Genoa, 1977); see, among others, the color plates XLI to XLIV, which are the most spectacular.

93. Exhibition catalogue *Kunst voor der beeldenstorm* (Amsterdam, Rijksmuseum, 1986), no. 155, pp. 278–79, repr. (discussion by C. Megan Armstrong).

94. After the review of the booklet of the Salon of 1873, no. 937, p. 145; at the same Salon, Lenoir exhibited another "exotic" work: *The Wise Elephant (Indian). The Siege of Pelusium* was sold at auction in New York on 6 October 1966 by Sotheby Parke Bernet (repr. in catalogue); its whereabouts are unknown.

95. Photograph in the "Cat" dossier at the Warburg Institute in London.

96. J. Raabe, *op. cit.*, vol. I, p. 314, late sixteenth-century German engraving: here the cats besiege •the

mice's citadel with its very Germanic towers and roofs; p. 312, sixteenth-century Dutch woodcut; pp. 256–57, eighteenth-century English woodcut.

97. J. Adhémar, *op. cit.*, no. 37, woodcut "A Lyon, chez Léonard Odet, 1610, au coin de la rue Ferrandière" (Paris, Bibliothèque nationale, Cabinet des estampes).

98. F. Tristan, *op. cit.*, fig. 57, satirical seventeenth-century French engraving (Paris, Bibliothèque nationale, Cabinet des estampes).

99. Jean-Claude Boyer, "Les Représentations guerrières et l'Évolution des arts plastiques en France au XVIIe siècle," *Revue du XVIIe siècle, Présence de la guerre au XVIIe siècle,* July–September 1985, no. 148, 37th year, no. 3, p. 297, repr. fig. 6: engraving by Jacques Lagniet.

100. Jean Lestocquoy, *Arras* (Colmar-Ingersheim, 1972), p. 90, repr. of engraving by Gabriel Pérelle (1600–1675).

101. Christabel Aberconway, *A Dictionary of Cat Lovers: XV Century B.C.—XX Century A.D.* (London, 1949).

102. Philip Hook and Mark Poltimore, *Popular 19th Century Painting: A Dictionary of European Genre Painters* (Antique Collector's Club, 1986), "Cats and Dogs" chap., pp. 114–41.

103. At the Ministry of Finance in Paris since 1890.

104. Paintings sold at auction, Hôtel Drouot, Paris, 7 March 1986, nos. 89–90, repr. (representing cats playing "in Napoleon's study").

105. Champfleury, *Les Chats* (Paris: J. Rothschild, 1868; republished in 1869).

106. François-Raphaël Loffredo, "Des recherches communes de Barye et de Delacroix au laboratoire d'anatomie comparée du Museum d'Histoire naturelle," *Bulletin de la Société de l'Histoire de l'Art français, 1982*, 1984, pp. 147–57.

107. Painting sold at auction, Sotheby's, London, 8 April 1981, no. 92, repr.

108. Élisabeth Foucart-Walter, exhibition catalogue *Les Peintures de Hans Holbein le Jeune au Louvre* (Paris, Musée du Louvre, 1985), pp. 48–49, repr. and p. 76.

109. Michèle Prouté, "Le Chat de Mademoiselle Dupuy," *Gazette des Beaux-Arts,* September 1979, pp. 95–96.

110. Gemma Cortese Di Domenico, *Una poetessa ed altri animali (Cronachetta romana del secolo XVIII)* (Rome, 1982), pp. 9–10, repr.

The dimensions of the paintings in the catalogue are given in inches.

STUDIO OF COSMÉ TURA

Active in Ferrara from 1431 to 1495

Virgin and Child
Panel. 17 1/2 x 12 3/4
Philadelphia, Philadelphia Museum of Art,
Johnson Collection

Here the Infant Jesus is not content merely to hold the little bird in his hand (as he is often shown in earlier works); he plays with it, holding it on the end of a string. The bird, a goldfinch, was chosen for its Christian significance. As its name in many languages indicates (the French *chardonneret* derives from *chardon*, thistle), this small bird is noted for its preference for thistles. That is why it has traditionally been considered an allusion to the crown of thorns and hence to the Passion. Thus, in holding the bird, the Infant Jesus is tied to his destiny—he cannot escape the Passion. The cat which has crept into the scene, unnoticed by the Virgin and Jesus, is a grave threat not only to the bird, which may not escape it in time, but also to all of mankind. Christ's sacrifice, with which humanity will be saved, must take place; thus the cat represents the world of Evil.   E.F.-W.

DOMENICO GHIRLANDAIO

Florence, 1449 — 1494

The Last Supper, 1481
Fresco. 165 1/4 x 307
Florence, Convent of San Marco

In the art of this period in Italy, it was customary to isolate Judas from Christ and the other apostles at the sacred table. Here Judas is deprived of his halo as well — but to place a cat with him, like an acolyte, was completely unprecedented. Ghirlandaio did just this at the refectory of San Marco, although he had never before included a cat in his depictions of the Last Supper. The cat's placement so close to the traitor has not escaped comment. In spite of everything, Ghirlandaio did not reduce Judas to utter baseness; he retains at least the dignity of Evil and the Animal. It has been rightly inferred that the cat represents the powers of Evil. Each of the birds likewise bears a Christian meaning. The peacock (at right) signifies Eternity, the pigeon (at left) the Eucharist, the partridges that streak across the sky are symbols of Evil; the fruit trees and the cherries sprinkled over the tablecloth signify Paradise before the Fall. The cat stares insistently at the viewer, taking no interest in the proceedings, as if it knows that nothing can interfere with the unfolding miracle and the impending betrayals of Jesus by Judas and Peter.   E.F.-W.

ANTONELLO DA MESSINA

Messina, ca. 1430 — 1479

Saint Jerome in His Cell, ca. 1474
Canvas. 18 1/4 x 14 1/4
London, National Gallery

A tiny grey tabby, in profile, turns its back to the saint: very early on, long before it was a companion to Baudelaire's scholar (see p. 89), the cat kept company with the sage. It shares in the silence and peace necessary to the seeker's concentration. Antonello seems to have had more difficulty painting the cat than he did the quail and peacock, which are rendered in minute detail in the foreground, or the lion that slowly approaches the saint. The cat, it must be admitted, adds very little to this lovely, crystalline work, which is monumental despite its small dimensions.   P.R.

49

COSIMO ROSSELLI

Florence, 1439 — Florence, 1507

The Last Supper, 1481
Fresco. 140 1/4 x 218
Vatican, Sistine Chapel

Like Ghirlandaio's Judas (see p. 46), painted during the same year, Rosselli's Judas partakes of the Last Supper alone on one side of the table, though here he retains his halo (not for long, certainly; the spirit of Evil in the form of a tiny demon already perches on his neck). On the ground a cat crouches, but unlike the placid cat of San Marco, it is locked in angry confrontation with that sworn enemy of its kind, a dog. Despite the overly smooth and polished finish that is characteristic of fresco, one senses the tension of the two snarling animals in the foreground, just next to the sacred vessels. Their confrontation can surely be construed as a battle between Evil (the cat, once more) and Good (the dog, which is faithful to its master, as the apostles are to Christ). To reemphasize the idea of faithfulness, another small dog to the left rears up, as if to bring itself nearer to its master. This is the only picturesque note in an otherwise austere composition without trees, fruit, or birds.   E.F.-W.

51

HANS SÜSS VON KULMBACH

Kulmbach, ca. 1480 — Nuremberg, 1522

Young Girl Weaving a Wreath
Panel. 6 1/2 x 5 1/2
False Dürer monogram and
false date of 1508
New York, Metropolitan Museum of Art

Seated in the window, and given equal prominence, are a girl and her pensive white cat. The animal watches the melancholy young woman plait a wreath of forget-me-nots, as the ornamental band indicates. (In Old German it reads, "ich pint mit Vergis mein nit"—"ich binde mit Vergissmein-nicht," that is, "I bind with forget-me-nots.") On the reverse side of the panel is a portrait of a young man. The meaning of this double-faced picture (a German specialty at this time) is clear: the forget-me-not is, of course, traditionally the flower of remembrance. The woman demonstrates her fidelity to her absent fiance or husband and shares a sorrowful solitude with her faithful feline companion, which also seems affected by its master's absence.

The French for forget-me-not—*myosotis* (derived from the Greek) means "mouse's ear," in reference to the blossom's shape. Had the cat been French, one imagines it might have shown less tranquility in the presence of this provocatively named flower.   E.F.-W.

HANS BALDUNG GRIEN

Schwabisch-Gmund, 1484/1485 – Strasbourg, 1545

Allegorical Figure of Music, 1529
Panel. 32 1/4 x 13 3/4
Munich, Alte Pinakothek

The viola de gamba—a very fine example of its kind, according to A. P. de Mirimonde—and booklet of songs identify this female figure as an allegorical representation of Music. The cat's presence has not yet been satisfactorily explained, although much ink has been expended in the attempt. This picture and its pendant in Munich (a nude woman stepping on a serpent, and looking in a mirror that reflects a skull and, in the background, a stag and a doe) are perhaps part of a series illustrating the Four Temperaments. If that is the case, the large, sleepily huddled white cat (certainly not the most handsome of animals), which is entirely indifferent to the rest of the scene, would symbolize the phlegmatic temperament, and the other allegory would represent melancholy. Or may we see in these two panels the contrast between Luxury (the nude female evoking Venus and the cat strengthening the allusion to voluptuous sensuality) and Virtue; or, perhaps, a parallel between the vanity of music and the vanity of existence?

E. F.-W.

DOSSO DOSSI

Ferrara, ca. 1489 — 1542

Holy Family with Donors, about 1515
Canvas. 38 1/4 x 45 1/4
Philadelphia, Philadelphia Museum of Art,
Johnson Collection

Roberto Longhi's attribution of this painting to Dosso Dossi, and its date, ca. 1515, are now generally accepted.

Is the animal actually a domestic cat? It might be a civet or genet cat, which were household pets in the Middle Ages (one sees them frequently in miniatures) but which, because of their penetrating, musky odor, were replaced in the fifteenth century by the domestic cat. Despite a certain clumsiness of execution that suggests the artist's unfamiliarity with the animal, it seems probable that Dossi intended to paint a domestic cat, especially as in religious pictures the cat is usually a symbol of Evil and is often associated with the goldfinch (see p. 45). P.R.

ITALIAN SCHOOL, EARLY SIXTEENTH CENTURY

Young Man with a Cat and a Dog
Panel. 11 x 9 1/2
Oxford, Ashmolean Museum

The identity of this model with his vague and melancholy gaze is as mysterious as that of the artist. Among others, the names of Domenico Mancini, Dosso Dossi, or one of Giorgione's followers have been suggested as possible authors of the work. The man holds a dog and cat—that is, we suppose that he does; his arms are outside the frame, an arrangement that only adds to the picture's pervasive strangeness.

The timeless character of the figure (the man is clad according to no recognizable fashion, his head wrapped in a strange turban like that of a Sybil) suggests that it was intended as an allegory rather than a mere portrait of an animal-lover. Thus we may conjecture that it is the antithesis of the allegory of Contrast (*Contrasto*), described by Cesare Ripa: a young man, armed either to defend himself or to attack is seen between a cat and a dog that confront each other, because, Ripa explains, contrast originates in what is fundamentally dissimilar by nature, and cats and dogs are eternal enemies. The peaceful young man shown here has succeeded in reconciling opposites and thus illustrates the idea of perfect harmony among the contradictions that make up human nature.   E.F.-W.

BACCHIACCA

Florence, 1494 — 1557

Portrait of a Young Woman Holding a Cat,
ca. 1525
Canvas. 21 1/4 x 17
New York, Art market

A somewhat wild-looking cat regards us with its paws delicately crossed on its lovely mistress's breast. One would like to know who these two are and why they are shown together. Representations of cats were still rare in sixteenth-century Italy and generally had a precise symbolic significance. It is tempting to see this work as an allegory of Sight (see p. 122). At the very least we can say that Bacchiacca, whose talents as an animal painter Vasari praised, did not intend simply to depict a family pet in its mistress's arms. The artist returned to this theme in another painting (Berlin-Dahlem), but in that picture the young woman, no less delicately, cradles a lynx. P.R.

LORENZO LOTTO

Venice, 1480 — Loreto, 1556

Annunciation, ca. 1527
Canvas. 65 1/4 x 44 3/4
Recanati, Pinacoteca civica

One of the most extraordinary cats in painting, this tabby that bounds across the center of the composition was not the only cat that Lotto painted. The artist had previously hidden another, with phosphorescent yellow eyes that glow from the shadows, in the background of *Christ Meeting with His Mother* (1521, Berlin-Dahlem).

Is the cat in the *Annunciation* at Recanati simply a gentle domestic pet terrified by the angel's arrival, or does it possess a symbolic meaning? Perhaps it is a symbol of Evil, the dark angel sent to announce that the Savior must die to redeem mankind.

Lotto has purposely stiffened the gestures of God, the Virgin, and the Angel. The only dynamic element in the composition is the conspicuous cat, which makes it all the more disquieting and mysterious.

Lotto himself warned us: he wanted his *Annunciation* to express *pensieri strani*—strange thoughts.   P.R.

58

59

PONTORMO

Pontormo, 1494 — Florence, 1556

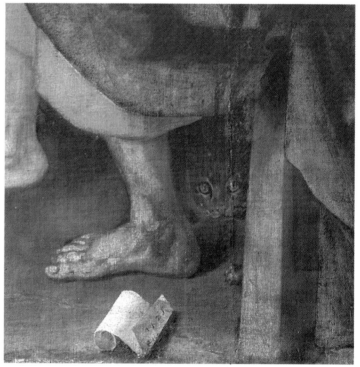

The Supper at Emmaus, 1525
Canvas. 90 1/2 x 68 1/4
Florence, Uffizi

Two cats (and a dog) at the extreme left and right of the composition beam their phosphorescent gazes at us. The presence of these realistic elements in this otherwise serious, ambitious work that focuses on the event's supernatural aspect remains a mystery. They may re-emphasize Christ's immortality, as Bernard Dorival has said of similar details in Philippe de Champaigne's work (see p. 108). In any case they are a disquieting note in one of the most powerful and innovative works of Florentine Mannerism. Pontormo's cats are contemporaneous with the animal in Lotto's *Annunciation* (see p. 58).   P.R.

61

GIULIO ROMANO

Rome, 1499 — Mantua, 1546

Madonna of the Cat
Panel. 63 x 56
Naples, Museo e Gallerie Nationali
di Capodimonte

All of the scene's participants turn to the Infant Jesus; only the cat looks straight at us. Does it warn us of the death of Christ? Its terrified and terrifying eyes hold all the misery of the animal chosen to represent Evil. Romano's cat is without question one of the most striking in the history of painting.

As is his wont, Romano plays up the contrast between the picture's minutely detailed realism—as in, for instance, the *trompe-l'oeil* marble flagstones—and its monumental conception and spiritual loftiness. But it is the intense presence of the cat that attracts and fascinates. That the picture has been named for it is only right.   P.R.

JACOPO BASSANO, called JACOPO DA PONTE

Bassano, ca. 1515 — 1592

The Supper at Emmaus, ca. 1538
Canvas. 98 1/2 x 92 1/2
Citadella, province of Padua, parish church

The Bassanos are without question the greatest sixteenth-century Venetian painters of animals: sheep and dogs, donkeys and cats occupy places of honor in the Bassanos' works (see, in this regard, Fernando Rigon's small work, published in 1983, on animals in Jacopo Bassano's *oeuvre*).

The cat of Citadella was long-lived: it appears to have survived at least until 1550, at which time Bassano executed his energetic, masterful *Last Supper* at the Borgia gallery. One easily recognizes it by the markings on its head and by the anxious expression it wears at the sight of the dog, which (the cat seems to feel) is sleeping very lightly.

In the Bassanos' works, for the first time in Italy, animals, particularly cats, were not relegated to the ranks of accessories but played equal parts with the human protagonists in the Biblical narratives.

P.R.

64

65

FEDERICO BAROCCI

Urbino, ca. 1535 — 1612

The Annunciation, 1582–1584
Canvas. 97 1/2 x 67
Rome, Pinacoteca Vatican

B arocci loved cats. He drew them frequently—preserved at the Uffizi in Florence is a series of drawings of all sorts of breeds in diverse poses—and sometimes painted them (the *Madonna del gatto* at London's National Gallery; the *Madonna della gatta,* very much damaged, in the Uffizi). As far as we know, no contemporaneous account mentions this passion of his. The cat in this *Annunciation* sleeps peacefully on a chair cushion. Why did Barocci choose to represent it this way, while Lotto imbued the cat in his *Annunciation* (see pp. 58–59) with such a precise negative meaning? We don't know—just as we don't know whether Barocci wanted merely to paint his own pet or meant to instill it with symbolic meaning as well. Barocci was one of the first artists to express an innocent affection for cats, possibly his own, in his works.   P.R.

66

VERONESE

Verona, 1528 — Venice, 1588

The Wedding at Cana, 1562–1563
Canvas. 2,622 x 389 3/4
Paris, Musée du Louvre

The picture is renowned, the cat less so, as it has escaped mention in the anthologies of "the cat in art," with their nearly always identical iconography. Lying on one side, a tiger cat claws at the mask decorating an amphora as it is attentively watched by a greyhound, which is fortunately leashed. The dog may symbolize servitude and the cat freedom. Whatever the case, such "dialogues" between two animals are not uncommon in Veronese's works (see *The Meal at the House of Levi* in the Galleria dell'Accademia in Venice and *The Supper at Emmaus* at the Louvre).

Rarely has an artist depicted a cat from the angle that Veronese chose here, as a demonstration of his virtuosity, and rarely has such finesse been brought to bear in depicting an animal at play. The cat is only one of a profusion of picturesque details that Veronese has scattered through this work without in any way distracting the viewer's attention from the scene's all-important miracle—Christ's transformation of water to wine.

P.R.

GEORG PENCZ

Nuremberg, ca. 1500 — Leipzig, 1550

Family Portrait, 1541
Panel. 63 1/2 x 47 1/2
Nuremberg, Germanisches National-
museum (on loan from the Bavarian State
collection)

Despite its title, this painting evokes that most Christian of themes, the Madonna and Child—transposing it to an interior that bears the stamp of the era's humanistic preoccupations. A medallion of Cicero hangs near the window and a Latin inscription appears on the wall behind the vase. The baby plays with an apple just as the infant Jesus would play with the fruit of Eden in a pre-figuration of His redemption of man-kind's sins. The second child, a little older, recalls the young John the Baptist; he amuses himself by blowing soap bubbles from a pipe, an obvious reference to the fragility of earthly things, as the bubbles will undoubtedly burst. There are other symbols of worldly vanity as well: the flowers, the empty glass, and on the table a rattle whose spiral may intimate the passage of time. The cat, a lovely animal, is far more than a mere domestic pet. Its sidelong glance at the goldfinch perched on the table, a reference to Jesus's crown of thorns, implies that a certain menace hovers over man's hope for salvation (as in the painting by Tura, p. 45).   E.F.-W.

70

PIETER BRUEGHEL THE ELDER

Breda(?), 1525/1530 — Brussels, 1569

Flemish Proverbs, 1559
Panel. 46 x 64 1/4
Berlin-Dahlem, Gemäldegalerie

In this illustration of almost 120 proverbs and popular sayings, the unusual exercise of belling the cat is carried out amid other examples of foolish and futile human activities. Behind the cat, a dreamer muses on the chicks to come, before any eggs have been laid; behind him, at the window, a monomaniac continually gnaws at the same bone while, in front, a lunatic bangs his head against the wall. The beller of the cat, in order to achieve his ends without being scratched, wears armor and grips a knife between his teeth as if to make clear that he is "armed to the teeth" (the knife does not appear in the numerous copies of this work by Pieter Brueghel the Younger, or by others after him—it is as if no one grasped its significance). The proverb's meaning is complex. It both castigates one who throws himself into a dangerous endeavor and denounces his cowardice at the same time—the man derives his courage from his armor, but the cat seems quite placid in any case. Besides, the consequences of such an act are difficult to foresee. The cat, once belled, will no longer be able to catch mice, which will then invade granary and home: Beware, then, of famine.   E.F.-W.

VINCENT SELLAER

Mechelen, ca. 1500 — 1589

*Jupiter as a Satyr with Antiope
and Their Twins*
Panel. 55 1/4 x 43
Paris, Musée du Louvre

Cats—especially cats like this fat feline, which seems to purr tranquilly as it serves as an armrest for a curly-haired boy as red-headed as itself—have not traditionally been associated with Jupiter and Antiope. Antiope, who was the Queen of Thebes, bore Jupiter twins, Amphion and Zethus (accompanied in this painting by two putti, in a kind of contamination from the Charity motif). No cat figures in the story, yet Sellaer included a cat in another painting of the same subject (Florence, Private Collection). Thus one may see in this animal as well a tactile sensuality and "a nice bit of soft, gentle reality that strikes us by the power of its visual presence," as Jacques Foucart has written. As such, the cat is very much in keeping with a depiction of Love through the loves of the gods.   E.F.-W.

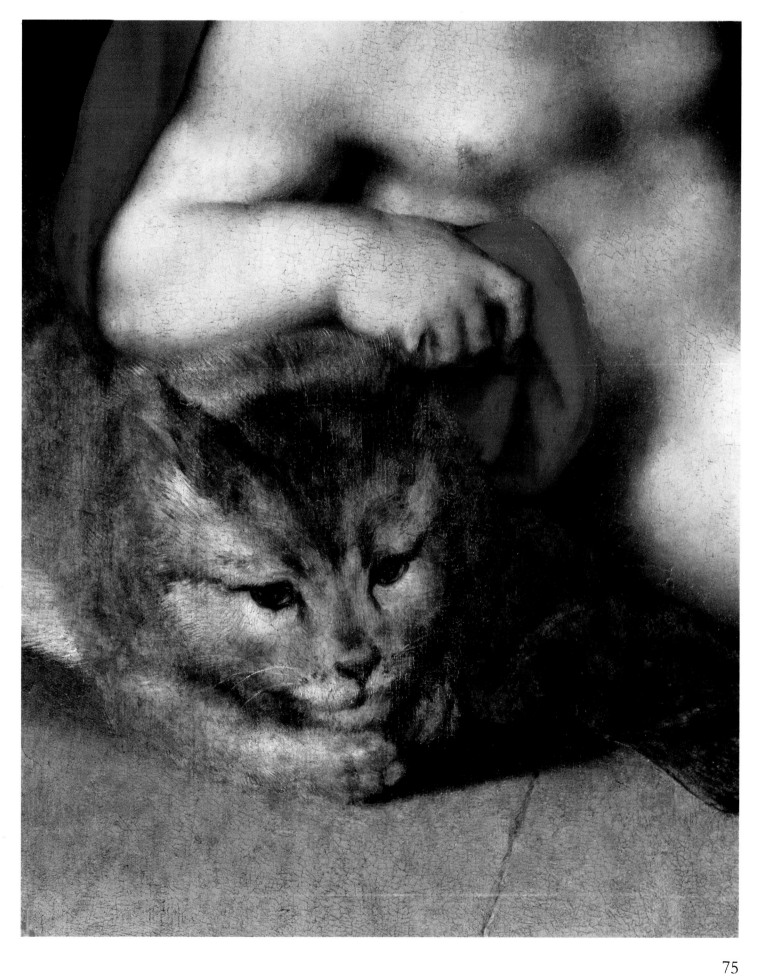

ATTRIBUTED TO PIETER AERTSEN

Amsterdam, 1508 — 1575

Display of Fruits and Vegetables
Panel. 40 1/2 x 53 1/4
Rotterdam, Museum Boymans-
van Beuningen

Cats have never been great admirers of fruits and vegetables, and the grey cat that appears at the back of the picture contents itself with sagely observing this veritable vegetable stew through a window, without getting too close. The dog prefers human company: it has joined one of the men, who strokes its head as he draws water from the well. The cat, placed as it is, cannot go unobserved in spite of its remoteness; the arm of the man seated on the wheelbarrow traces a sinuous line that inevitably draws our gaze back to the cat. In a typically Mannerist way, the painter has juxtaposed the elements within different planes to create a somewhat oppressive illusion of depth and weight. The gigantic cluster of grapes that looms up in the foreground seems out of all proportion to the man's face nearby, and even more so in comparison with the cat, which is reduced to the size of a mere handful of these grapes.

E. F.-W.

MAERTEN VAN CLEVE

Antwerp, 1527 — 1581

T aking advantage of the chaos that reigns throughout the scene, a cat nestles for a short nap in a comfortable wicker cradle, momentarily empty; simultaneously, its confederate, to the right in the background, sups from the same dish as some young children. Cats aren't the only animals embroiled in this delicious confusion—there is a dog, of course, along with some chickens and pigs, and cows, which can be seen to the right in the background. All share the cottage on equal footing with humans. The cat, which seems so indifferent to the doings of the others, man or beast, could never pass unnoticed, placed as prominently as it is. This picturesque motif is frequently found in paintings of this period: sometimes it is a dog lying in a cradle, in a somewhat surprising role as a kind of hermit-crab, a concrete embodiment of the overall good humor and harmony (peace among humans, and between man and animals) that such scenes exude.   E. F.-W.

78

Flemish Interior, ca. 1555–1560
Panel. 48 1/2 x 56 1/2
Vienna, Kunsthistorisches Museum

JAN CORNELISZ VERMEYEN

Beverwijck, near Haarlem, ca. 1490–1500 — Brussels, 1559

The Holy Family
Panel. 26 x 19 1/2
Vienna, Kunsthistorisches Museum

In this scene, where the figures, in a typically Mannerist way, seem to tip out toward us, a simple wood fire casts a strange glow. Only Joseph, who warms his hands high on the left, and the cat sleeping on the cloth have closed their eyes: the former because he has not yet been touched by the Revelation, and the latter perhaps for that reason, but mainly because it is comfortably sleeping near the hearth. Two other persons look straight towards us: to the right, a turbaned woman bends forward, and across from her a little angel turning around towards us, holding a cloth before the fire in a gesture that prefigures Saint Veronica's. Jesus, on His mother's lap, has surely seen the cat. He seems to point to it with his left hand, but does not look at it; his eyes are lifted heavenward. The animal is not placed so much to the fore sheerly out of whim (although it seems the painter was very fond of cats: he put two in the foreground of a 1545 engraving of an Oriental woman). It is a symbol of the forces of Evil that the Son of God, mankind's savior, will vanquish.   E.F.-W.

OTTO VENIUS

Leyden, 1556 — Brussels, 1629

Otto Venius Painting, Surrounded by
His Family, 1584
Canvas. 62 1/4 x 98 1/2
Paris, Musée du Louvre

Venius, shown at his easel, did not hesitate to include the house cat in this portrait of the family. Unfortunately, although he took care to put a little number above each person's head (these are invisible in the reproduction) corresponding to a name on the list inscribed on the cartouche to the right, Venius neglected to give the cat a number, and thus it will ever be nameless. The animal is obviously pleased to be stroked by a little girl named Elisabeth and seems very civilized and peaceable in comparison with the primitive and savage cat holding a bird in its jaws, which can be distinguished on the tapestry just above the easel.

E.F.-W.

CORNELIS CORNELISZ VAN HAARLEM

Haarlem, 1562 — 1638

Adam and Eve, 1592
Canvas. 107 1/2 x 86 1/2
Amsterdam, Rijksmuseum

It is a very singular pair that occupy a strategic position at the foot of the Tree of Knowledge of Good and Evil, just beneath the fatal apple, which Eve has offered to Adam. Durer had already coupled Adam and Eve's sin with a cat—his celebrated 1504 engraving may have inspired Van Haarlem—but the cat in Durer's work dozes, without monkey or other companion. Van Haarlem's strange painting has inspired numerous interpretations. The tenderly embracing animals could represent two of the four temperaments—the cat signifying the choleric temperament, and the monkey the sanguine. These temperaments supposedly existed in perfect harmony before the Fall. (In that case, the dog would symbolize the melancholic and the slugs the phlegmatic temperaments, respectively.) Or perhaps the cat and monkey represent the threatening apparitions of sensuality and lewdness, respectively. All the other animals in the scene would possess specific meanings as well (for example, the butterfly poised on the tree trunk between Adam and Eve would represent the soul's frailty). But the painting may also be a simple depiction of an ideal universe in which the animals lived together in peace, before they became mortal enemies. Like the dog, the fox, the sheep, the hedgehog, the frogs and slugs, the bear and the lion, the two affectionate animals are sharing the last minutes of a happiness that will be forever shattered by the Fall.   E.F.-W.

ATTRIBUTED TO PIETER WTEWAEL

Utrecht, 1596 — 1660

Vanity
Panel. 43 3/4 x 35 1/2
London, Art market

An elegant young woman seated before an ornately framed mirror contemplates her reflection, which reveals an infinite sadness that her profile gives no hint of. At her side, a solemn young man, hat held negligently in hand, leans familiarly over her chair and also gazes at her image. The only creature that turns away (and the only one depicted frontally) is the cat. Pawing insistently at its mistress's hand, it regards her anxiously, mewing—almost certainly in warning. Will it scratch?

The scene's import is as strange as the atmosphere it exudes, as complex as the play of gazes and hands that sustain this flawlessly Mannnerist work. Is the man a seducer—has he bestowed the gem that the woman wears on her brow? Her melancholia, so evident in the mirror, might express a more general idea of the vanity of female beauty and the futility of wordly preoccupations (represented by the toilet articles—the comb, powder puff, and scissors, the jewels and the mirror itself, with its over-luxurious frame). These pastimes are all the shallower as they are perceived only through so fragile and transient object as the mirror. The cat's role is unclear. It may want to bring its mistress back to reality—to distract her from too much reflection (in which case its role is dubious), or it may seek rather to warn her of the perils of seduction (in which case it would be her guardian angel). It is possible that we witness two self-centered characters in conflict—the cat, which feels abandoned, and the young woman, who is locked in contemplation of her image. Whatever the animal's aim, its success is not assured: for the moment, the man and woman pay it no mind.　　　　E.F.-W.

87

GIOVANNI LANFRANCO

Parma, 1582 — Rome, 1647

Naked Man Playing with a Cat in Bed,
ca. 1620
Canvas. 44 1/2 x 63
London, Art market

Only one thing is certain about this work, which is in poor condition: it is by Lanfranco. It belonged to Queen Christina of Sweden, who died in Rome in 1689; and to Philippe d'Orléans, who attributed it to "Horace Gentileschi" before it was sent to England with the d'Orléans family's collection.

Judging by the portrait medallion that adorns the account of the painter's life in Bellori's celebrated *Vite,* it is doubtful that the man is Lanfranco himself.

The picture is meant to shock: an young man, entirely naked and barely covered by a sheet, stretches along an unmade bed, turning toward us with a smile. He strokes a large, very ugly black-and-white cat—probably his own. Why this scene, and why such an affectionate feline? We are at a loss. Seventeenth-century Roman painting is full of surprises.   P.R.

PIETRO PAOLINI

Lucca, 1603 — 1681

Writer with a Small Cat
Canvas. 22 1/2 x 26
Lucca, Former Guinigi Collection

Lovers most passionate, scholars austere
    Both love, when their autumnal season falls,
Strong, gentle cats, majestic, beautiful;
They, too, sit still, and feel the cold night air.

Baudelaire, "The Cats" *Baudelaire: Selected Poems,* 1975

A bas-relief, or rather grisaille, of Apollo and the Muses crowns the bust of our poet. A little gray-and-white cat perches on the shoulder of the writer, whose laborious concentration and studious isolation proclaim him—as in Baudelaire's description—a scholar. The animal observes its master's mysterious pastime with surprise and quizzical amusement.

P.R.

GIOVANNI BENEDETTO CASTIGLIONE

Genoa, 1609 — Mantua, 1663/1665

Noah's Sacrifice
Canvas. 22 1/2 x 31 1/2
Genoa, Palazzo Bianco

Of all the Biblical scenes, Noah's sacrifice before boarding the Ark is particularly well-suited to the depiction of animals, but cats are very often forgotten. Castiglione, a great animal painter, chose the theme many times (examples exist in Vienna, Los Angeles and elsewhere) and always included cats in his pictures.

The Genoa version shows the pairs of animals assembling as the sacrifice unfolds to the right in the background. A ginger and a gray-and-white cat in the foreground turn toward us without any indication of apprehension or of interest in their fellow travelers.

Castiglione renders them faithfully, but with no more sympathy than he does the sheep or the parrots.   P.R.

GIUSEPPE RECCO

Naples, 1634 – Alicante (?), 1695

Cat Stealing a Fish
Canvas. 37 3/4 x 50 1/4
New York,
Metropolitan Museum of Art

A handsome grey tabby is being surprised in the act of devouring an octopus. Rendered with great verisimilitude, the cat regards us fearlessly, an tentacle dangling from its jaws. We have disturbed it in its larder, stocked with the gleaming fish in which Recco specialized.

The association between cat and fish is classic—the former, as all know, are mad for the latter. Their encounters have been depicted on innumerable occasions, particularly by the seventeenth-century Dutch painters, and no lengthy explanation is required here.   P.R.

BERNHARDT KEIL

Elsinore, 1624 — Rome, 1687

Girl with Fan and Cat
Canvas. 19 1/4 x 37 3/4
Private Collection

Looking a little anxious and sad, the small girl holds a fan of the kind made in sixteenth-century Italy, when an engraving (often containing a short tale) was often inserted into the wooden framework. The child is accompanied by a cat with big, bright eyes. Its slight hostility echoes the scene's odd, indefinable strangeness and melancholy. This canvas has a pendant in which a young boy slumbers profoundly beside a cat that is also asleep. The meaning of both pictures is obscure (W. Sumowski is content to remark that they are problematic). They may simply be representations of the opposing states of sleep and wakefulness. The text on the fan is too faint to help us: only its first two words, "AMORE DIO . . ." are decipherable. Perhaps the girl, awaking to life, invites the hazards and pain that the god of Love will inflict upon her. If the small picture engraved in the middle of the fan is, as we think, a horse, it would support the interpretation: in traditional iconography a horse frequently accompanies Eros. Meanwhile, the young boy sleeps "the sleep of the just," safe in his oblivion. But sleep signifies night, and to some extent, death; it is not associated with bliss or comfort here. The waking state is no less futile; as long as one lives, one cannot escape the torments of love. As for the cats in the two scenes, they reinforce the contradiction between these two children. It is tempting to imagine that one cat is a female and the other a tom. 　　　　　　　　　　　　　　　　　　　　E.F.-W.

DIEGO VELÁZQUEZ

Seville, 1599 — Madrid, 1660

The Weavers, also known as *Making the Tapestries of Santa Isabel in Madrid*, ca. 1657 (?)
Canvas. 86 1/2 x 113 3/4
Madrid, Prado

This painting's numerous interpreters—whose constructions have incorporated many elements, from the legend of Arachne to that of the virtuous Lucretia's spinning, and have ranged into the most complex neo-Platonic speculations—for the most part have made nothing of the cat sleeping in the foreground, partly hidden by the woman at the spinning wheel. Observers who mention the animal reduce it to a simple compositional motif. Only J. H. de Azcárate's analysis assigns a truly major role to the cat (and is included herein for that reason alone). According to Azcárate, *The Weavers* is a political painting designed to exalt obedience to the Spanish monarchy and elicit repentence in rebel breasts. The cat's presence is said to demonstrate that obedience is the opposite of servitude, since the cat, which will not tolerate captivity, is the very emblem of liberty. This idea is set forth in treatises by both Cesare Ripa and Valeriano, and the inventory of Velázquez's library indicates that he possessed both works. Thus this simple, furry ball—which is almost indistinguishable from the pincushions and whose long, strong shadow along the ground forms part of the painting's subtle play of light—would attain an almost royal symbolism in this studio full of bustling women. It is doubtful that a great painter such as Velázquez would put himself through such iconographic contortions.　　　　　　　　　　　　　　　　　　　　　E.F.-W.

BARTOLOMÉ ESTABAN MURILLO

Seville, 1618 — 1682

The Holy Family, before 1650
Canvas. 82 1/4 x 65
The Hague, Royal Palace

The little grey striped cat—not yet fully grown—is shown at the same age in another of Murillo's paintings of the Holy Family (Dublin, National Gallery), and is thus ancillary proof that the two paintings are contemporaneous, a conclusion Murillo's historians had already arrived at solely on the basis of style while entirely ignoring the cat and its implications.

Curled up on the straw chair, it sleeps, taking advantage of Mary's pose as the Virgin of Humility, seated on the ground. This is in contrast to the Dublin picture, in which Mary has taken a seat on the chair and the cat casts her a vexed glance at having been dislodged.

Such cats are certainly present for a reason: they satisfy more than the very Spanish taste for a realism which expresses the sacred through the language of everyday life. Murillo was too familiar with Christian iconography not to use the cat in his depiction of Christ's infancy. It appears as an emblem of the trials the Son of God would undergo to save humanity.

E.F.-W.

JACOB JORDAENS

Antwerp, 1593 — 1678

The King Drinks, ca. 1640–1645
Canvas. 95 1/4 x 118
Vienna, Kunsthistorisches Museum

In this vast depiction of the banquet traditionally enjoyed in Flanders during the celebration of Epiphany (at the cry "The King drinks!" the king of the revels lifts his glass to his lips), Jordaens has shown at the foot of the royal chair—the place of honor—an enormously fleshy, furry cat, whose puffy features remind one strangely of the congested face of the drunken monarch of the day. The cat is slightly isolated within the composition, so that, reproduced in detail, it looks almost like an entirely separate picture. Holding some food in its claws, the sated feline regards us with narrowed eyes, while a neighboring dog seems more interested in the spectacle of a guest vomiting.

In this scene, which is dominated by the moralistic (or perhaps ironic) inscription *Nec similius insano quam ebrius* ("Nothing resembles a fool more than a drunkard"), the huge cat can bear no innocent significance. As the only quiet guest amid the joyful company, is it not a mocking denunciation of humanity's excesses? In this scene, it is the animal that is wise, and man who is mad, not to say bestial. E.F.-W.

98

REMBRANDT

Leyden, 1606 — Amsterdam, 1669

The Holy Family, also known as
The Carpenter's Household, 1640
Panel. 16 1/4 x 13 1/2
Paris, Musée du Louvre

A mid the shadows one makes out with difficulty the figure of a tabby drowsing by the fireplace. It is there nevertheless, just like its fellow in the *Holy Family* in Kassel (1646), or like yet a third cat in a 1654 engraving entitled *Holy Family with a Cat*. This is one of the few cats in Rembrandt's paintings; rather, dogs of all sizes and shapes throng his canvases. The master chose the silent, discreet cat for this most intimate scene from Christ's childhood. The Virgin, her mother Anne, and Joseph are gathered about the baby Jesus in their modest interior, near the cat that is encountered in every household. It need not be assigned a particular meaning. Rembrandt's greatness and originality lie in his transcendance of traditional iconography, his transformation of established symbols—through the alchemy of his realistic brushwork—into familiar details that have no need of any further explication. Here, the sacred has become commonplace: we assume that the book St. Anne has set aside along with her glasses is simply the Bible. The yoke that Joseph fashions in his corner is certainly a Biblical allusion to the prophecy of Isaiah (the Savior will break the yoke of Israel), but it has become an ordinary object; by the same token, the cat, that baleful and oft-feared animal, is nothing more than a harmless pet warming itself next to a pot from which tempting aromas waft. Details great and small unite in Rembrandt's magical, intimate world.   E.F.-W.

JAN MIENSE MOLENAER

Haarlem, ca. 1610 — 1668

Children Playing With a Cat
Canvas. 26 x 21 1/4
Dunkirk, Musée des Beaux-Arts
(permanent loan of the Louvre)

We must not let ourselves be put off guard by the two children's insoucience: the girl's gesture in pointing at the cat, the only "person" who looks straight at us, is charged with meaning. An explanation is supplied by an inscription on an engraving after a painting (rightly attributed to Judith Leyster, Molenaer's wife) that presents in the same manner two laughing youngsters with a cat. Such a scene bears in fact a moral import: earthly joys and worldly pleasures are ephemeral and can be rudely interrupted (by sickness or death) just as the children's laughter and games could be halted by a cat's scratch. This occurs in another of Molenaer's paintings (at the Musée d'Épinal) in which the little cat—apparently the same as in this picture, and most certainly the painter's pet—turns its claws on the child's chest, drawing blood. The velvet paw has become hostile and cruel, and the child's laugh will soon become a doleful wail.

E.F.-W.

102

JUDITH LEYSTER

Haarlem, 1609 — Heemstede, 1660

Young Man With a Cat
Panel. 17 3/4 x 17
Kassel, Gemäldegalerie

This is not just a portrait of a young man holding a cat in his arms and keeping its head very straight and still so that it will not move out of the field of the painting; it is also a portrait of the cat, which is so vital that we expect to hear it mew at any moment. Its little eyes as bright as its master's, the young cat stares at us cheekily, for all the world like one of Frans Hals' saucy boys, commanding our attention. Its mouth stretches in a raffish grin emphasized by the whiskers that only reinforce its astonishing resemblance to its master: the mischievous cat and the jeering scamp are comrades in laughter and mockery.

Judith Leyster and her husband Jan Miense Molenaer were both very fond of cats, judging by the many pictures each did in which felines appear on an equal footing with people. E.F.-W.

FRANS SNYDERS

Antwerp, 1579 — 1657

Still Life with Cats
Canvas. 38 1/2 x 54
Private Collection

From their earliest youth, Snyders' cats are wont to make their way into kitchens and onto tables and buffets loaded with food. Thus, in the foreground of a large painting at the Musée des Beaux-Arts in Lyon, we see three small kittens grappling with dead birds almost as big as they. In other of Snyders' canvases, adult cats squabble savagely over fowl and game (as, for example, in the painting at the Pinacothek in Munich; this has often been copied, notably by Paul de Vos who did an enlargement that is now at the Prado in Madrid).

The duel between the two animals (one no doubt a she-cat, with a calico coat, and one a tom) doesn't seem to center on gastronomical concerns, as there is nothing among the precious gold vessels, or the vegetables and fruits, that would interest them. Snyders, like the good Baroque painter he was, sought to suggest movement even in the inanimate objects through a clever play of dynamic curves. Thus he chose to depict the precise moment at which the basket is tipping, although we cannot surmise where it stood before the drama began. The cats' undulating bodies and tails interlink in spirals that echo the curves of the objects; only the table, walls and window form right angles in contrast to the rest of the composition. A third cat, at the very edge of the picture, makes for an amusing visual diversion.

E.F.-W.

JAN FYT

Antwerp, 1611 — 1661

Cat Studies
Canvas. 33 x 43
Vienna,
Akademie der bildenden Künste

These are not five different cats, but all the same animal—a lovely, muscular, irregularly mottled beast—that Fyt has represented in diverse poses. Such studies, as independent works are rare, even exceptional, during this period. Boel did them a bit later (see p. 118), but it was Desportes, even later, who became the master of the genre (see pp. 128–29). The study's repertoire of feline forms and attitudes is employed by the painter in depicting the numerous cats that inhabit his vast still-life compositions. These animals, rarely immobile and always observed with astonishing precision, poise ready to bound toward a bird or some dead game, or to scrap with a dog as thieving as themselves, meowing and twisting about like the cat on the right, which seems to threaten an invisible enemy from its post at the foot of the oak tree. The harmonious distribution of the five studies across the wooded escarpment (itself an unrealistic touch, as the cat does not seem at all wild) confers on the canvas an air of unity and completeness that renders it all the more captivating.   E.F.-W.

LE NAIN

Louis (Laon, 1593 — Paris, 1648?)

Peasant Family in an Interior
Canvas. 44 1/2 x 62 1/2
Paris, Musée du Louvre

Cats are common in Le Nain's works, and their presence, not at all decorative, is never without purpose. In the center of the picture, a little white cat with black spots hides behind an earthenware tripod and lid. Immobile, indifferent to the dog, it regards something that is invisible to us. It seems to listen to the flageolot's music with the peasants, partaking of the solemn, noble poetry so characteristic of Le Nain's works.

P.R.

PHILIPPE DE CHAMPAIGNE

Brussels, 1602 — Paris, 1674

The Supper at Emmaus
Canvas. 85 1/2 x 89
Ghent, Musée des Beaux-Arts

How can one not feel surprised at the austere painter of Port-Royal having placed, in the foreground of this most sacred scene, a small tabby cat with no interest in anything save the vessel that contains the meal's leftovers? This is far from a simple, familiar detail, although in other renderings of the Supper at Emmaus (see pp. 60–61 and 64–65), cats peer timidly from behind the guests' legs. According to Bernard Dorival, this impudent cat has a precise symbolic meaning based on a sixteenth-century commentary on hieroglyphics. The cat is the hieroglyph for the moon and its corollary, "the beginnings and endings of things." Its presence at Emmaus reminds us that "the risen Christ will never die." How impious, then, is the servant who, with no respect for such an august symbol, is about to shoo the cat away with a sweep of his hand.

E.F.-W.

MICHEL CORNEILLE

Orléans, 1603 — 1664

Esau Selling His Birthright to Jacob, 1630
Canvas. 45 1/4 x 49 1/2
Orléans, Musée des Beaux-Arts

Esau sells his birthright to his brother Jacob for a pot of lentils that Jacob has prepared. Meanwhile, a sad, small, dirty white cat, astonished and fascinated, discovers its own reflection in the shining lid of the copper cauldron in which the lentils have cooked.

Corneille has skillfully played off the contrast between the two domestic animals, in an interior which is that of a French bourgeois home of about 1630.   P.R.

CHARLES LE BRUN

Paris, 1619 — 1690

The Infant Jesus Asleep,
also known as
Silence, 1655
Canvas. 34 1/4 x 46 1/2
Paris, Musée du Louvre

Originally, the cat was not the only animal in this scene, if we are to judge by an aged copy (formerly at Potsdam) which shows John the Baptist cradling a squirrel in the crook of his right arm. This animal, Fouquet's emblem, was distinctly unwelcome at the time the picture entered the collection of Louis XIV, and hence was effaced. Even by itself, the cat, comfortably ensconced under a brazier just beside the painter's monogram *C.L.B.*, is too evident to be anything but proof of a discreet realism, even if modern commentators continue to see it as a mere descriptive element. The feline's quiet doze reinforces the painting's general import, which has to do with the mystery of the Word incarnate. The Virgin hushes the turbulent young John the Baptist so that Jesus (the Word of God) will not be awakened; it is necessary to avoid warning Christ of His Passion before its time is at hand.

Just so, an old French dictum advises us to "let sleeping cats lie," for fear of the dangers that might attend their awakening—proof that Christianity's tenets and popular wisdom can sometimes agree, even when cats are concerned.
E.F.-W.

GOVAERT CAMPHUYSEN

Gorinchem, 1623/1624 — Amsterdam, 1672

Cat and Pigeon in a Window,
between 1652 and 1663
Canvas. 37 x 29 1/4
Private Collection

The significance of this un-heard-of tête-à-tête between a very peaceful cat and a pigeon in an open window is not known. Per-haps one day a proverb or symbol will surface to explain it. We only know, thanks to the painter's sig-nature, which is conspicuous on the white paper by the red curtain, that the picture was painted in Stock-holm, where Camphuysen lived for a decade beginning in 1652. More-over, several of the town's gables and steeples rise in the background.

The casket holding a precious pearl necklace, and the casket key on a yellow ribbon can be interpreted along with the watch suspended in the embrasure as symbols of the vanity of coquetry, and more generally, the fragility of appearances in the face of fleeting time. The cat, which seems to be the guardian of the earthly treasures, may be the counterpart of the bird, which could signify the immaterial spirit or the soul's immortality. The animals' indifference to one another gives little indication as to which will pre-vail, the flesh or the spirit. The bird may fly off, abandoning the cat to its useless treasure and to ridicule.   E.F.-W.

114

DAVID TENIERS THE YOUNGER

Antwerp, 1610 — Brussels, 1690

Cat Concert
Panel. 10 1/4 x 12 1/4
Munich, Bayerische
Staatsgemäldesammlungen

The theme of animals as musicians is as old as music itself. The idea is not merely a pretext for amusing artwork; it also possesses satirical import. Thus, in this concert-parody (also called *Concert Miaulique*), does not Teniers—reportedly a great music-lover and musician—mock his contemporaries' mania for making music, often very badly? Six cats—three large, three small—have climbed up on a table and are singing at the tops of their lungs as they beat time with abandon. Before them, an owl, figuring as a conductor, perches upon a fat music book. On the floor are two tiny monkeys, one playing a chalumeau. Other instruments (lutes, a bagpipe) are not yet in use. The only listener, a cat, pokes its head in through the window, doubtless drawn by the clamor. Let it be noted that in Flemish, Teniers' language, the word *Kattenmusik* (literally, "cats' music"), means din or racket.   E.F.-W.

CORNELIS DE MAN

Delft, 1621 — 1706

The elegant tabby, with its red belled collar that matches the table rug, is perfectly at home in this rich, neat interior. It turns with interest towards the pair of chess players, gazing at the gesture the young woman makes to the viewer, inviting us to watch her next move. The cat also accords well with the scene's underlying meaning. The game of chess—in which planning prevails over chance—can refer to the game of Love, a game as pitiless as that of the cat with the mouse. This plump cat would be a wretched hunter, its every move betrayed by the tinkling bell—but let the mice beware lest an enemy hand (for them it would be the hand of Fate) remove the cat's collar.   E.F.-W.

116

Chess Players, ca. 1670
Canvas. 38 1/4 x 33 1/2   Budapest, Museum of Fine Arts

PIETER BOEL

Antwerp, 1622 — Paris, 1674

Studies of a Wild Cat
Canvas. 16 1/4 x 10 1/2
Paris, Private Collection

B oel, who must have been a student of Fyt, has gathered here five studies of the same cat's head viewed from different angles: two versions straight on (and inverse to one another), one in profile, one from below and one from above, the last two being particularly unusual. The difference between Fyt's cat (see p. 105) and this one—which wails ferociously with bared fangs and shaggy fur (a detail that lends itself particularly well to Boel's free style of execution)—is that this animal definitely has the air of a wild cat. Boel was a specialist in animal sketches: as part of the process of making Gobelin tapestries, he created borders of flora and, above all, fauna. He also did numerous animal studies (often confused with those of Desportes [see pp. 128–29]), whose models were the exotic inhabitants of the king's menagerie as often as they were the beasts of the forest or field.

Cats in Boel's work appear in many guises, and are always well served by the painter's frank style of observation. A canvas very similar to this one (attributed to Salvatore Rosa) is at the Accademia Nazionale di San Luca in Rome; an equally virtuosic and purposeful study at the museum in Alençon shows four views of the same cat (not wild this time, but no more reassuring for all that). Finally, since the eighteenth century the Hermitage has possessed a double of this last study, more flatteringly attributed to the great Snyders, and with a false signature. One doesn't know whether this hoax was prompted by a passion for cats or the love of painting.   E.F.-W.

118

ABRAHAM HONDIUS

Rotterdam, 1625/1630 — London, after 1695

The Monkey and the Cat
Canvas. 24 1/2 x 28 3/4
Cleveland,
Cleveland Museum of Art

The proverbial phrase about "pulling chestnuts out of the fire" refers to taking a risk for another's sake without any profit to oneself. It originated in one of Aesop's fables, retold by Phaedrus and, of course, by La Fontaine (whose first edition is dated 1671), who described the scene in this way: the monkey persuaded the cat that the latter's talent for retrieving roasted chestnuts from the fire was unsurpassed. Flattered, the cat bent its skills to the task, but without much reward: the monkey devoured the chestnuts as quickly as the cat pulled them out.

This indeed takes place in Hondius's painting, except that the monkey, the better to gain its ends, guides the unfortunate feline's paw into the glowing coals, making the cat scream with pain. It is a cruel detail and spurious besides—it is not part of the fable—and it has a counterpart in Hondius's predilection for ferocious hunting scenes and animal fights. In the final analysis, the fable's moral vanishes in favor of an anatomical (and, indeed, psychological) study of the two animals, above all the cat, whose pained, almost human expression contrasts with the monkey's greedy gaze as the very sharply observed chestnuts, their hulls split open with the heat, roll about on the ground. E.F.-W.

119

JAN STEEN

Leyden, 1628 — 1679

The Reading Lesson
Panel. 17 3/4 x 13 3/4
Basel, Kunstmuseum

In the kitchen, under the eyes of a young serving maid, three children give a reading lesson to their pet cat: it is the only one present that shows no appreciation for this eminently pedagogical effort.

A pendant (now at the Fine Arts Society of San Diego) to this scene shows the same three youngsters spooning gruel into the cat (now dressed up in doll clothes). This time the animal seems blissful. The moral lesson of these genre paintings is clear: physical pleasures, such as eating, are easier to obtain than the spiritual elevation gained from learning, reading, or teaching. In another such scene, some children teach a kitten to dance (Amsterdam, Rijksmuseum).

Under the guise of this pleasant game in which animals enact human roles, Steen conceals an irony that parodies even his own works: his School-Master (Dublin, National Gallery) is just as severe towards an unfortunate student as is this young mistress towards her disciple, whom she threatens with a small switch. E.F.-W.

120

121

BARENT FABRITIUS

Midden-Beemster, 1624 — Amsterdam, 1673

Sight, ca. 1666
Panel. 15 1/2 x 13
Aix-la-Chapelle, Suermondt Museum

As all the world knows, cats see equally well by night and by day. Nothing could be more natural, then, than that they should figure in allegorical depictions of Sight, such as the celebrated engraving by Jan Saenredam after a work by Hendrick Goltzius (1616), in which Venus regards herself in a mirror held up by Cupid while a cat, crouched in the foreground, displays its complete indifference to the scene (see p. 16). In the small painting above, part of a series of works (all at Aix-la-Chapelle) that depict the Five Senses, Fabritius gives the principle role to the cat (it seems to be a calico, very pleased with its looks), which takes Venus's place in the traditional language of allegory. Nevertheless, the young boy must hold the animal firmly by its hind paws, a well-considered detail, since it is difficult (as those who have tried know) to keep a cat still for long in a pose not of its own choosing.

E.F.-W.

EGLON HENDRIK VAN DER NEER

Amsterdam, 1634 — Düsseldorf, 1703

Children with Caged Bird and Cat
Panel. 8 1/4 x 6 3/4
Karlsruhe, Staatliche Kunsthalle

Van der Neer's scene is not just a depiction of the cruel play of two naughty well-born children, who are worthy of inclusion in one of the Countess of Segur's moralistic tales. The bird that they are forcing out of its cage and toward the cat's deadly claws has a very precise meaning. One may refer to an emblem by Daniel Heinsius (1615) in which a mouse cowering in a mousetrap is stalked by a cat, under the eyes of a little Cupid armed with a bow and arrow. The caption, a sonnet by Petrarch, ends thus: "If I remain in captivity, I remain in peril, if I free myself, I run toward death." The meaning is clear: the cage is Love, which takes one captive; but in escaping to freedom the prisoner faces a still graver danger—Death, embodied by the cat that Van der Neer's youngsters must incite to attack its prey. Hence the moral: there is no salvation outside of Cupid's chains.   E.F.-W.

123

NICOLAS MAES

Dordrecht, 1634 — Amsterdam, 1693

The tranquility of this scene of deep devotion is endangered by the presence of a mischievous, greedy cat that, mocking all "peace of God," tugs at the white tablecloth with the claws of its right paw.

Once again, we must ask whether the feline is only a familiar domestic element in a depiction of daily life. Indeed, cats, so as not to be excluded from blessings, are generally discreet. It may, however, play a more complicated role, in its willingness both to upset the objects on the table and also to disrupt the woman's unfolding prayer. According to Paul Claudel, who was well aware of the cat's mischief (*The Listening Eye,* 1938), this painting harbors both "immobility and movement, a state of equilibrium undermined by unrest in the form of the cat's avid paw." E.F.-W.

The Blessing. Canvas. 52 3/4 × 44 1/2. Amsterdam, Rijksmuseum.

WILLEM VAN MIERIS

Leyden, 1662 — 1747

Woman Talking with a Fish-Monger, 1713
Panel. 19 1/4 x 16 1/4
London, National Gallery

Has this lovely calico cat been tricked by the *trompe-l'oeil* bas-relief into thinking one of the winged putti is a new kind of bird? Or does it gaze, with a more practical eye, at the dead duck that dangles over the ledge? Here, as in other, similar works, Van Mieris places a live animal (which seems to exist more in the viewers' space than in the scene itself) against a bas-relief, playing up the contrast between the cat's silky fur and the stone's cold smoothness. In a similar vein, the artist's *Kitchen Stove* (Paris, Musée du Louvre) shows a magpie busily pecking at some carrots that have tumbled to the ground, while in the *Grocer's Shop* (The Hague, Mauritshuis) a rat gnaws at some grain that has dribbled from a sack. All of these animals pursue their own ends completely oblivious to human concerns.   E.F.-W.

FRANÇOIS DESPORTES

Champigneulles, 1661 — Paris, 1743

Two Studies of a Young Cat
Oil on paper. 10 1/2 x 20
Cambridge, Fitzwilliam Museum

In 1784 Nicolas Desportes sold the king all of the studies from his uncle's studio, which he had inherited. Animals are depicted in most of the studies, but some vegetables appear, and the work is generally in oil on paper. Most of them have remained in the French national museums, but some, such as this (which was long attributed to Jean-Baptiste Oudry), have surfaced elsewhere.

Better than any photograph, Desportes' study captures the cat's motion, the mobility of its paws, the play of its muscles, and its terrified expression (see also pp. 105 and 118). For Desportes, cats were only a vehicle, a pretext—they could as easily be wild boars, or greyhounds. The artist used his studies as preliminary sketches in creating his paintings of game, but they are so keenly observed in their own right that in addition to admiring their decorative qualities one cannot but be seduced by Desportes' virtuosity as an observer of nature.　P.R.

129

PIERRE SUBLEYRAS

Saint-Gilles du Gard, 1699 — Rome, 1749

The Falcon, after 1732
Canvas. 13 3/4 x 11
Paris, Musée du Louvre

Subleyras preferred cats to dogs; nonetheless, he well understood the dog which, as it gnaws a bone, turns toward its master so as to share in the proceedings. The scene is inspired by La Fontaine's famous story in which a young woman at last yields to her suitor's entreaties after he sacrifices for her his most precious possession, a falcon. Its inert form is visible on the lovely white table cloth.

Crouched on a wooden chair, the prettily spotted cat is lost in its own world. It seems indifferent—is it truly, or does it eavesdrop on the lovers, undetected? Whatever the case, its presence lends palpable tenderness and warmth to the scene. P.R.

130

131

JEAN-BAPTISTE SIMÉON CHARDIN

Paris, 1699 — 1779

The Laundress, ca. 1733
Canvas. 14 1/2 x 16 1/2
Stockholm, Nationalmuseum

As an example of a cat by Chardin (he was a great cat lover, judging by his paintings) one would expect to find the artist's renowned *Ray* (Paris, Musée du Louvre) reproduced here. The cat in the *Ray*, we confess, is not our favorite Chardin cat. Slipping like a burglar into that sumptuous still life, it is still too reminiscent of the Flemish seventeenth-century cats to do full justice to Chardin's genius. Our apologies. We prefer the calico cat in *The Laundress,* painted about 1733, a cat that, we are certain, belonged to Chardin from 1728 on. Like the little boy engrossed in his play with the soap-bubble, like the young women who scrub and hang up the linen, the cat is painted at a standstill. The people and the cat, all self-absorbed, at once near to each other and far away, partake of the marvellously shy and human intimacy of which Chardin is the poet.   P.R.

CHARLES-JOSEPH NATOIRE

Nîmes, 1700 — Castel Gandolfo, 1777

*Portrait of Louise-Anne de Bourbon, called
Mademoiselle de Charolais,* after 1730
Canvas. 46 1/2 x 35 1/2
Versailles, Musée national du Château

Mademoiselle de Charolais, a great-granddaughter of Louis XIV (her grandmother was born of the king and Madame de Montespan), enlivened the court's chronicles with her very turbulent way of life; she was also said to be occasionally devout. Perhaps that is why Natoire depicted her dressed as a monk and tying knots in her girdle. This prompted Voltaire to say: "Brother Angel of Charolais / Tell me by what surprising chance / The cord of Saint Francis / Doubles as Venus's belt." Unfortunately, the ironical writer made no reference to the cat that is so very much in evidence. In this otherwise pleasantly artificial portrait (books, papers, writing pen and cup are placed in an outdoor setting), this little animal is in fact the most genuine detail. As the provocative young woman ties her knot in an offhanded, graceful way, averting her gaze the better to take her gallant prey by surprise, the cat looks straight into our eyes and openly kneads with its claws at a luxurious cushion that was, one hopes, given to it for that purpose.   E.F.-W.

FRANÇOIS BOUCHER

Paris, 1703 — 1770

The Beautiful Country Maiden
Canvas. 16 3/4 x 12 1/2
Pasadena, Norton Simon Collection

Boucher specialists will readily recognize this cat with its speckled ears, curiously thick black eyebrows and spotted nose. It appears in one picture after another for a decade, first very young (*The Surprise*, Museum of New Orleans), then older and larger. Finally, one day, it is replaced (*The Dressing Table*, Lugano, Thyssen Collection).

Tenderly Boucher has observed this dreamy little boy who is absorbed in playing with his cat as his mother watches. For the artist as for his contemporaries, the cat held really no further symbolic meaning.

P.R.

JEAN-JACQUES BACHELIER

Paris, 1724 — 1806

Angora Cat, ca. 1761
Canvas. 25 1/2 x 35 1/2
Paris, Private Collection

Bachelier exhibited this painting at the Salon of 1761, under the title *Angola (sic) Cat Stalking a Bird.* As a pendant the artist painted *A Poodle Exercising* for the architect Soufflot. One of the Salon's commentators admired in this cat "those very secret stirrings of appetite excited in it by a canary, which has flown too close to it not soon to become its prey."

Bachelier clearly delighted in painting the cat's sumptuous silken fur, long plumed tail and bushy, drooping whiskers. Angora cats had been recently introduced into France by the erudite Nicolas-Claude Fabri de Peiresc (1580–1637), himself a great lover of cats (Pierre Humbert, *Un amateur, Peiresc...*, Paris 1933, p. 148). He obtained them in the Levant, after hearing descriptions of pure white cats with "long, frizzy hair like a water spaniel's, whose tails, uplifted, form the loveliest plumes ever seen..."   P.R.

JEAN-BAPTISTE PERRONNEAU

Paris, 1715 – Amsterdam, 1783

Woman with Cat, 1747
Canvas. 26 x 20 1/2
Malibu, J. Paul Getty Museum

The enormous elephant-gray animal glares ferociously at us with gray eyes: its mistress holds it still with difficulty. Is it incensed because of its belled collar? Whatever the reason, it is clear that Perronneau intended to portray the cat as much as its mistress. She also wears a collar, but hers is of pearls.　　　　　　　　　　　　P.R.

139

JEAN-BAPTISTE GREUZE

Tournus, 1725 — Paris, 1805

The Winder, 1759
Canvas. 29 1/2 x 24
New York, Frick Collection

An innocent cat? Who could doubt it, seeing its attentive gaze as its mistress winds a ball of yarn? But anyone who knows Greuze would want to delve further into his intentions. The young white cat, mottled with yellow and brown, plays with a strand of the yarn and thus impedes the girl's concentration on her work. She dreams. Of what? Of whom? The cat may well symbolize the kind of distraction that sometimes leads to grievous consequences for a young girl's virtue.

P.R.

140

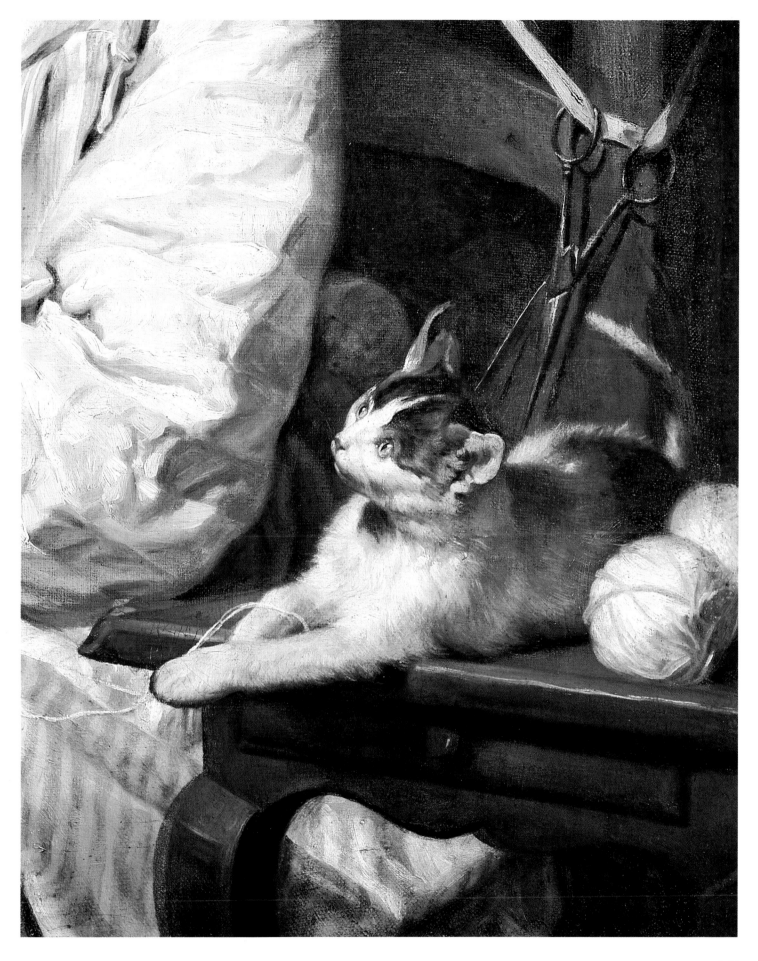

PHILIPPE MERCIER

Berlin, 1689 — London, 1760

Young Girl Holding a Cat, ca. 1745–1750
Canvas. 35 3/4 x 27 1/2
Edinburgh, National Gallery of Scotland

Animals—particularly cats—have long occupied a privileged place in English painting. With few exceptions (notably Hogarth's painting [see pp. 158–59]), the subjects of these works are young women or girls who affectionately cradle their pets in their arms. Curiously, one of the first of these sentimental renderings is the work of a French painter, a follower of Watteau (from afar) who was born in Berlin and settled in London.

Also unusual is the fact that Mercier was not afraid to depict a black cat, despite the prejudice against such animals. The complicity between the girl and her young companion, and their resemblance to one another, which the painter has emphasized, lends the picture its considerable charm.   P.R.

142

JEAN-HONORÉ FRAGONARD

Grasse, 1732 — Paris, 1806

Young Girl Holding a Dog and a Cat
Round canvas; diameter 27 1/2
Tel Aviv, Private Collection

This masterpiece by Fragonard has been identified (without great proof) as a portrait of one of the Colombe sisters, dancers who enlivened Parisian annals of the 1780s. In it a young girl holds a puppy and a white kitten with blue eyes in her arms, observing with slightly perverse interest the impending struggle.

Cats are common in Fragonard's works. Nonetheless, he preferred bulls or pedigree dogs, and only rarely accorded cats a prominent place (see *The Music Lesson* at the Louvre and, above all, *The School Mistress* in the Wallace Collection in London). P.R.

JEAN-FRANÇOIS-GILLES COLSON

Dijon, 1733 — Paris, 1803

Repose, 1759
Canvas. 36 1/2 x 29 1/2
Dijon, Musée des Beaux-Arts

The titles of this painting and of its counterpart, *Action* (Private Collection), seem simple enough, but they do not tell all. An oddly marked young cat is surprised at the moment it is preparing to pounce on a canary that its mistress holds by a ribbon. In comparison with the treacherous animal, which attempts to profit by the drowsy girl's inattention and devour the innocent bird, the valiant spaniel in *Action* is shown assisting its young master as he prepares to fire a toy cannon.

It is evident that the cat which abuses its sleeping mistress's confidence is once again playing a less than admirable role. It has, at least, engaged the painter's sympathy.
P.R.

144

145

NICOLAS-BERNARD LÉPICIÉ

Paris, 1735 — 1784

Fanchon Awakes, 1773
Canvas. 29 1/4 x 36 1/2
Saint-Omer,
Musée de l'Hôtel Sandelin

With lashing tail, a cat greets its mistress who, sitting on the disordered bed, pulls on a stocking. The cat, purring, rubs affectionately against her leg.

Is this a simple genre painting—a straightforward depiction of a servant's room, or a roguish tableau that lingers complaisantly over the charms of a rather wanton young woman? The scene's sensual ambiguity, bolstered by the presence of the cat, is intentional. Each viewer must decide whether the animal is a domestic pet or an emblem of luxury. P.R.

FAUSTINO BOCCHI

Brescia, 1659 — 1741

Dwarves Caring for a Cat
Canvas. 27 1/2 x 39
Private Collection

Cats are a part of Bocchi's fantastical, grotesque world: along with rabbits, chickens and guinea pigs, they are maltreated by a race of bustling dwarves, many of whom are legless or walk about on stilts, turbaned or no. Here, a sick cat is about to be purged (enemas, for both humans and animals, are frequently depicted in Bocchi's works). The doctor and apothecary (the latter bewigged and bespectacled) have climbed up onto a table, as if they were in a play by Moliere. From there they spout opinions, consulting a large book, larger, no doubt, than the sum of their knowledge. Bocchi executed another painting on this theme (Italy, Private Collection): its pendant shows dwarves towing a sick cat in a wooden cart up to a bust of some ancient divinity (Pan?), whom they entreat to heal it. The cats are similar—spotted, with a very melancholy, almost human air. Long nosed and down in the mouth, they share in the ugliness of Bocchi's sickly, absurd world, in which animals and humans are used to mock one another.   E.F.-W.

148

ITALIAN SCHOOL OF THE EIGHTEENTH CENTURY

Cat and Dog in a Window
Mural
Naples,
Convent of San Gregorio Armeno

W e do not know the creator of this exceptional *trompe-l'oeil* work. It was executed simultaneously with the completion of the interior of the cloister of San Gregorio Armeno in Naples, for which almost fifty years earlier Giacomo del Po (1659–1726) had painted a Saint Benoit in glory. The painter of this sham window amused himself by facetiously placing on the sill and hence on the exterior, a cat and dog. The animals are somewhat naive in style (especially the cat, with its tiny head), and the more comical for that. The window is situated just to the left of the church door, protected from bad weather by the cloister, and the two companions are posted like sentinels, observing all who enter or leave the church. How did they get up there? The cat could climb, but not the dog. No doubt the window had been opened to allow the two comrades to enjoy some fresh air. In any case, they seem to get along miraculously well together, and set a good example for the faithful, who must, perforce, be moved to establish harmonious relations with one another.   E. F.-W.

GIUSEPPE MARIA CRESPI

Bologna, 1665 — 1747

Young Girl Teasing a Cat with a Rose Stem
Canvas. 26 x 22
Bologna, Pinacoteca nationale

The picture is said to be a pendant of the *Young Girl with a Dove* at the City Art Gallery of Birmingham: the dove's softness would provide a counterpart to the rose's thorns and the cat's claws. Cats appear frequently in Crespi's genre scenes and religious compositions. His *Marriage at Cana* at the Art Institute of Chicago was directly inspired by Veronese's version (see pp. 68–69). One senses that Crespi loved cats. He so delighted in depicting their trusting abandon, their games and skittish independence, that their presence, rather than being decorative, is an essential element of his pictures. P.R.

GIACOMO CERUTI

Piacenza, 1691 — Brescia, after 1760

Little Girl Holding a Cat in a Basket
Canvas. 21 1/4 x 16 1/2
London, Art market

The black and white cat regards us steadily from the wide wicker basket. It is anxious, judging by its pricked ears, wide eyes, and extended claws. The little girl—her precocious coquetry evident in the rose in her hair—has opened the panier to show us her friend. As a pendant Ceruti painted a little boy in a tricorne hat, holding a bulldog that affectionately licks his cheeks.

Cats often accompany the wretched people that Ceruti painted so frequently. In his celebrated, heart-rending picture in the National Gallery at Brescia, one of two cripples delicately holds a very young kitten—the only tender note in a harsh portrait of human solitude.

This young lady inhabits a completely different world, however, and Ceruti had no other ambition than to portray the charming little girl and her playmate.   P.R.

GASPARE TRAVERSI

Naples, 1722 (?) — Rome, 1770

C ats are never absent in Neapolitan painting. They appear more or less discretely, in the secular as well as sacred works of Giordano, Solimena, and Francesco de Mura, and occupy a place of honor in Traversi's pictures. In *The Concert,* treated in the mordant, grating caricatural and realistic style that is the artist's own, a plump feline listens, ears pricked, to music played by a cellist, a flutist, and a young female harpsichordist with a sullen, disdainful face. The "music-lovers" who surround them seem more entranced by the lady than the music.

This white cat with several grey blotches must have belonged to Traversi: it is depicted full-face in his *Secret Letter* at the Museo e Gallerie Nazionali di Capodimonte in Naples.   P.R.

The Concert
Canvas. 59 1/2 x 80 1/4
Kansas City,
Nelson Atkins Museum of Art

JOSÉ DEL CASTILLO

Madrid, 1737 — 1793

The Painter's Studio, 1780
Canvas. 41 1/4 x 63
Madrid, Prado Museum

C ats are known for their independence, which verges at times on insubordination: the mascot of this atelier—probably Castillo's own—is certainly an exceptional beast in condescending to perform circus tricks.

It is a large cat, almost disproportionately so compared with the boy who plays with it, and its presence in the studio is enough to distract the artists from their drawing (they copy a tapestry cartoon for the apartment of the Princess of the Asturias at the Palace of Pardo). Apparently the cat was a specialist at jumping (a rarity!). The moment of calculation, of preparation for the leap is a welcome element in a painting that is on the whole a static spectacle. It is sharply observed, as anyone knows who has seen a cat thus poised to spring.   E.F.-W.

FRANCISCO GOYA

Fuentetodos, Aragon, 1746 — Bordeaux, 1828

*Portrait of Don Manuel Osorio Manrique
de Zuñiga,* 1788
Canvas. 50 x 43 3/4
New York, Metropolitan Museum of Art
Jules Bach Collection

Three stout cats fixedly eye a magpie held on a string by the little boy. Goya painted cats only rarely; these are rightly among the most famous in all of art. Does the bird represent the soul threatened by the Devil? And the goldfinches in a cage— a superb green cage that contrasts with the boy's red clothes—are they symbols of Innocence? The painting may depict the fragile world of childhood threatened by the forces of Evil. We do not know whether Goya consciously intended that any meaning be read into the work.

The three felines—a calico, a gray tiger and a black cat whose eyes glow in the shadows—are observed with penetration and humor (witness the painter's visiting card, which the magpie so visibly holds in its beak). With consummate psychological insight, Goya has captured the cats' cruel expectation, their careful concentration, their frustrated gluttony and mistrustful complicity. One feels that the painter harbored no great sympathy for them.   P.R.

156

WILLIAM HOGARTH

London, 1697 — 1764

The Graham Children, 1742
Canvas. 63 3/4 x 46 1/2
London, Tate Gallery

158

H ogarth may very well have been bored with painting children. Here, in any case, he has devoted all of his ironical attention to the tabby cat that clings to the back of the armchair and avidly contemplates the panicky bird in its cage. The cat's eyes, shining with lust, and its erect, trembling whiskers and half-open mouth through which one glimpses its tongue and fangs, are observed with acuity and humor. The cat's aggressiveness is laid bare, as is Hogarth's corrosive ferocity— a ferocity that in this case is tinged with warm forebearance.   P.R.

THOMAS GAINSBOROUGH

Sudbury, Suffolk, 1727 – London, 1788

A Child with a Cat
Canvas. 59 x 47 1/4
New York, Metropolitan Museum of Art,
Marquand Collection

Gainsborough painted many dogs and few cats, but those cats he drew were very handsome. In his picture at the Metropolitan Museum, executed just before his death, a fat calico accompanies a young boy who has just wakened and seems completely surprised to find himself in a strange forest. Why a cat—why *this* cat, which seems wild but is not at all frightening? We do not know. Perhaps it is there to render the composition less banal, less insipid.   P.R.

161

ATTRIBUTED TO JOHN HOPPNER

London, 1758 — 1810

Young Woman with Her Son,
Who Holds a Cat in His Arms
Canvas. 50 x 38 1/2
Paris, Musée du Louvre

The attribution of this work to Hoppner is occasionally contested. Indeed, the painting is not without clumsiness in execution and composition, but the young cat redeems the work by bringing a delicate note of tenderness to it. Above all, its presence permits the artist to convey the feelings that unite this young mother and her son, at the same time as he captures the modest reserve that is the very essence of the feline character.

P.R.

JOSEPH WRIGHT OF DERBY

Derby, 1734 — 1797

Dressing the Kitten
Canvas. 35 3/4 x 28 1/4
Kenwood (London), on loan from the
Iveagh Bequest

By the candle's glimmer, two little girls are dressing a kitten in the clothes of a doll that lies abandoned on the table. The picture is startling: the lighting, and the two friends' *décolletés* and costumes recall canvases by the Caravagesque painters of the Utrecht school. The painting's quasi-monochromatic coloration with its reddish mauves and gamut of browns, the transparent light, and the highlights on the girls' cheeks, noses, and lips recall comparable scenes by Gerrit van Honthorst.

Astonishing also is the subject—dressing the cat—which became very popular only in the nineteenth century. The kitten seems not in the least appreciative of all the pains being taken on its behalf. Wright may have seen this work as a moralistic lesson, as well as an excuse for glitteringly virtuosic brushwork: it is nearly a pastiche. The two young girls may soon turn to other, riskier games. P.R.

164

MARGUERITE GÉRARD

Grasse, 1761 — Paris, 1837

The Cat's Luncheon
Canvas. 24 x 19 1/2
Grasse, Musée Fragonard

Cats are not always welcome in Fragonard's pictures (one thinks of his *Music Lesson* at the Louvre), and they seem not to have engaged the painter's sympathy (see caption p. 143). In his sister-in-law's works, however, they are given pride of place. There are not many paintings by Gérard—from *Minette's Triumph* to *Prelude to a Concert*—in which cats do not play a primary role. Occasionally, as here, they are the subject of the picture: under the envious eyes of a dog, a cat receives a dish of coveted milk from its pretty mistress, who respectfully kneels before it. In truth, this splendid calico Angora (a breed very rare in France at that time), merits such considerate service. P.R.

MARTIN DRÖLLING

Oberhergheim, 1752 — Paris, 1817

The Woman with a Mousetrap, ca. 1798
Panel. 10 x 13 3/4
Orléans, Musée des Beaux-Arts

A handsome white Angora (for another example of this type, see p. 138), a little surprising in this modest interior, fervently eyes an inaccessible mouse. In the picture's pendant—also at the museum at Orléans—a young man holds a bone out to his dog. It is unnecessary to delve for obscure metaphysical meanings or complex symbolic innuendos in this work, but the artist has, nevertheless, associated the woman and the cat according to the code that was universally understood in the eighteenth century and which derived from Northern painting of the previous century.

Like the baby sitting in his little chair, the cat gazes, attentive but powerless, at the mousetrap. Will it finally gain the mouse that the young woman teasingly withholds? In the pendant, at least, there is no guile: the dog's master gives his pet its meal without delay.   P.R.

166

JEAN-FRANÇOIS GARNERAY

Paris, 1755 — Auteuil, 1837

Portrait of Ambroise-Louis Garneray,
the Artist's Son
Canvas. 26 1/4 x 21
Versailles, Musée national du Château

C lad in a picturesque red vest, Ambroise-Louis Garneray (1783–1857) affectionately hugs a superb white and gray Angora (whose fur is almost as long as the boy's hair, and is softer as well), and simultaneously grasps its right paw. The animal sits as if posed on a beautiful small marquetry table and stares straight ahead, its golden eyes expressing a certain irritation in contrast to the amused blue eyes of its young master. If this portrait is the one exhibited at the 1793 Salon, Ambroise-Louis would be shown at age ten, which is not impossible. The painting must have been executed before 1796, when the young Garneray left his family to embark on a frigate and begin an adventurous life as a mariner (he would be shipwrecked, held prisoner, and would encounter Surcouf). He abandoned this swashbuckling existence some twenty years later, returned to Paris and became a painter—of marine landscapes, naturally. The cat's career was no doubt less haphazard. It appears in a later Garneray picture, its small grey nose standing out against its white muzzle as it assists at a little girl's piano lesson. E.F.-W.

LOUIS-LÉOPOLD BOILLY

La Bassée, Nord, 1761 — Paris, 1845

Portrait of Gabrielle Arnault as a Child
Canvas. 8 1/4 x 6 1/4
Paris, Musée du Louvre

L ouis-Léopold Boilly painted all of the relatives of writer and Secretary of the Académie française Vincent Arnault (1766–1834), who was the cousin of the painter's second wife. A descendant bequeathed seven of these portraits of Arnault family members to the Louvre in 1904.

Here the writer's daughter Gabrielle, later Mme. Donat d'Aries, is shown with her cat on her lap. A magnificent Angora, the cat has long, silken, somewhat dishevelled fur that contrasts with the child's bare arms and her smooth, round face framed by a bonnet that permits not the slightest lock of hair to escape. The somewhat agitated animal seems impatient to end the pose and casts a sidelong glance with eyes as round as its young mistress's. Their two gazes gleam with the same brilliance, as if the painter had wanted to emphasize the rapport between the animal and the little girl, whom it is careful not to scratch in spite of its contrariness.

The painting's harmony of brown, beige and creamy white seems to have been conceived as a whole, centering on the cat's fur, which to a certain extent lends the work its tone. Several years earlier Boilly painted the model's older brother Louis (1803–1885) at the same age as Gabrielle; he was accompanied by two dogs whose large, round, shining eyes compelled immediate recognition as having been painted "à la Boilly" (Paris, Musée du Louvre). We will never know whether the artist was deliberately accentuating an innate resemblance between man and beast (one would say that this little girl, with her clear, astonished stare, could not but pick out a cat with marble-like eyes such as her own, or those of a doll), or whether Boilly was merely imposing the unifying stamp of his style.   E.F.

SWISS SCHOOL (?), NINETEENTH CENTURY

The Cat and the Goldfinches
Canvas. 14 1/2 x 18
Rouen, Musée des Beaux-Arts,
Baderou Donation

Here once again, the cat is associated with goldfinches, those tiny fowl seen so often in pictures of the Virgin and Child as foreshadowing Christ's Passion. But here there is no Christian symbolism— only a realism that is rather naive, but all the more charming for that. Against an Alpine background a cat, whiskers quivering (a detail familiar to those who have seen cats on the prowl) looks longingly through a window at two tame goldfinches, one of which seems to be picking up grain with the aid of a tiny pail. The lovely red-headed birds are perhaps insufficiently wary; the window pane is broken (doubtless an artifice contrived by the painter in order to indicate the otherwise invisible glass—as in a *trompe-l'oeil* by Boilly or the interiors of Drölling or Duval Le Camus), and the cat could reach in with a cruel, agile paw. E.F.-W.

FRIEDRICH OVERBECK

Lübeck, 1789 — Rome, 1869

Portrait of the Painter Franz Pforr, 1810
Canvas. 24 1/2 x 18 1/2
Berlin, Staatliche Museen Preussischer
Kulturbesitz, Nationalgalerie

In this portrait, as Gothic as one could wish, in accordance with Pforr's intentionally archaic artistic vision, the cat is surprisingly important. Its pose gently echoes the window's arch and serves as counterpoint to the equally curved figure of the young woman (Pforr's wife) who seems to have stepped straight out of a High Gothic Annunciation. And since Pforr's wife is present, this cat must be the family pet. Every detail has a more or less Christian significance: the woman's *Weinrot* (wine red) costume, in conjunction with the bunches of grapes, refers to the Eucharist; Pforr's emblem (a skull surmounted by a cross), which is carved under the window, signifies the victory of the Resurrection over Death; and the tame falcon, according to scholars, is a symbol of Hope. In this case the little Nazarene cat, the delicate mottling on its coat following the very formalized curves of its body, could also be connected to an iconographic tradition: the *gatto della Madonna*. The following year Pforr depicted the same cat in a religious painting—the "primitive" diptych *Mary and the Shulamite* for his friend Overbeck (Schweinfurt, Schäfer Collection)—in which the cat is associated with the image of the Virgin. E.F.-W.

ALEXANDRE-GABRIEL DECAMPS

Paris, 1803 — Fontainebleau, 1860

Bertrand and Raton, 1847
Canvas. 15 x 18
Château-Thierry,
Musée Jean-de-la-Fontaine
(on loan from the Musée du Louvre)

As its title indicates, the picture illustrates La Fontaine's fable of Betrand the monkey and Raton the cat—the fabulist invariably dubbed his cats Raton, perhaps in derision, or Raminagrobis. The scene, treated without the cruelty of Hondius (see p. 119) or Landseer (see p. 175), exudes La Fontaine's deceptive good nature. The two animals, who live under the same roof, are not enemies but accomplices in folly; one is, when the occasion presents itself, a little cleverer. The cat's graceful gesture, well observed by Decamps—who specialized in animals, especially dogs and monkeys—is taken from the text: "...Raton, with his paw, / in a delicate manner, / Pushes back the ash a little bit, / then pulls back his toes, / Then sticks them in again many times; / Pulls out a chestnut, then two, then three, that swindler..." The scene's realism is firmly established by diverse objects around the fireplace, but also by the point of view, which is at ground level, as if the onlooker were on all fours behind the two animals.

One remarks the elegance of the monkey's white-collared red vest and the cat's sparkling white fur, which even the coal does not besmirch. These details doubtless suit the story's moral, which is at once very aristocratic and fairly subversive—the monkey symbolizes the king. In royal circles similar tricks were often played on princes "who, flattered into like employment, / Are fleeced in the provinces / For some king's profit."

E.F.-W.

EDWIN LANDSEER

London, 1802 — 1873

The Cat's Paw, ca. 1824
Canvas. 29 1/2 x 27 1/2
Private Collection

The fable of the monkey and the cat, which inspired Hondius's ferociously naturalistic work (see p. 119), is taken up here by the English painter Landseer, a great animal specialist. The scene is no longer a hand-to-hand struggle, but rather an almost theatrical *mise-en-scène*: the monkey, dressed as a little man, and the cat, wrapped in cloth that hinders more than protects the unhappy animal, carry on in a riotously untidy room. In the background a curtain flaps beside an open window (through which, say commentators, the monkey must have come, an escapee from some circus). On the stove, close to the chestnuts, sits an iron; on the ground are scattered the shards of a broken pot and a lemon slice. Two smaller cats, certainly members of the duped feline's family, try in vain to defend their comrade.   E.F.-W.

Cats Before the Hearth Canvas. 18 x 23 1/2. Compiegne, Musée National du Château

THOMAS COUTURE
Senlis, 1815 — Villiers-le-Bel, 1879

T his lovely composition, rarely reproduced, is part of the group of Couture's paintings that his grandson Colonel Bertaux-Couture donated to the French museums in 1954. As with most of the works in this gift, it reveals a less well known, more intimate Couture, painting in a style very different from the declamatory academicism with which he has too often been linked.

Three cats crouch near the hearth in a bourgeois home—probably that of the painter, who lived at Senlis from 1859 to 1869, and after that at Villiers-le-Bel. A reddish light bathes the brown interior. The cats, edged with somber outlines and treated in a rapid, vigorous, almost slap-dash manner, become purely painterly motifs, like the superbly lit armchair or the mantlepiece. The cats' forms, almost indistinguishable from the container at the corner of the fire, are simple, even stylized, in an audacious manner that would be lauded as miraculous if it occurred in a work by Daumier or Couture's most renowned student, Eduard Manet, whose cats are more decorative but in reality less "modern" than these.   E. F.-W.

GUSTAVE COURBET

Ornans, 1819 — La Tour de Peilz, Switzerland, 1877

The Artist's Studio, 1855
Canvas. 141 1/4 x 235 1/2
Paris, Musée d'Orsay

P rominently in the center of his masterpiece, Courbet has placed a splendid white Angora, which plays gracefully with a maybug or other insect.

Margaret Armbrust Seibert, shunning the trend towards farfetched speculation, has proposed many convincing interpretations. She invokes, pell-mell, the book *Les Chats* (published in 1869 but undertaken twenty years earlier) by Champfleury, the writer, critic and friend of Courbet; and Cesare Ripa, according to whom the cat, which sees so well at night, is the emblem of clear vision. Above all, Seibert reminds us that during the Revolution the cat was a symbol of Liberty—and Liberty had to be draped in white. That Courbet would have awarded the animal so eminent a spot is thus not at all surprising.

Therefore, we must suspect that Courbet's cat, far from being innocent, forms one of the elements to be considered in a reading of *The Artist's Studio.* The surprise lies not in how well the artist was able to disguise his intentions, but that in spite of his intentions he sacrificed nothing of the quality of the painting itself. The cat, captured in motion, the staccato play of its paws admirably observed, is one of the masterpieces of the genre.   P.R.

179

JEAN-FRANÇOIS MILLET

Gruchy, 1814 — Barbizon, 1875

The booklet of the 1861 Salon (at which *Waiting* was exhibited) very fortunately contains anexplication of this scene. At first glance it seems more rustic than sacred; but Millet's great idea was to retell the stories of the Bible *en sabots* (in clogs). "Tobias's mother eagerly left her house each day, looking in every direction and traveling all the roads she hoped he would come back on, in an attempt to espy his return from afar." What, then, is a cat (of which there is no mention in the Biblical text) doing in the middle of the scene, between the mother searching the horizon and the blind, stumbling father whose sight Tobias will soon restore? Is not the cat "only, truth to tell, a rather anecdotal and ridiculous detail," as Andre Fermigier has said? Examine it carefully: it arches its back with a yowl, as if facing some enemy—a dog, for instance. According to the tale, in addition to his young wife Sarah and an angel, Tobias was accompanied by his faithful dog. The sacred book does not mention it, but is it not this animal that our cat has sensed from afar? This small detail illustrates Millet's thorough familiarity with the Bible. Besides that, the cat is essential to the story. It is a character in and of itself admirably observed, surely the most active and vigorous of the three, and, because of its cry, certainly the hardest to ignore.

E.F.-W.

Waiting, 1860–1861
Canvas. 33 x 47 1/2
Kansas City,
Nelson Atkins Museum of Art

JOHN EVERETT MILLAIS

Southampton, 1829 — London, 1896

The Flood, 1870
Canvas. 39 x 57 Manchester, City Art Gallery

The waves bear an unusual vessel, a cradle that holds an infant and a black kitten, an unexpected passenger that danger has compelled to climb up on board. The scene depicts an event that occurred in Sheffield after a dam had burst (Alma Tadema painted it also, but her cat screeches with terror). The little English Moses, unaware of his peril, takes obvious pleasure in the sight of the birds in the branches above his head, while the cat is too terrified to notice them. The birds are goldfinches, often associated with cats in scenes that allude to Christ's Passion: this may be an indication that Millais wished to inject a symbolic meaning into the scene. In that case, the cat, with its vociferous cries, would play an essential role, guiding the babe's saviors, shown approaching in the background, to the cradle.

The two models for the story (which had a happy ending) have been identified. The infant was Sophie, one of Millais's daughters, and the cat belonged to his friend, the painter Fred Walker.   E.F.-W.

183

WILLIAM HOLMAN HUNT

London, 1827 — 1910

The Awakening of Conscience, 1853
Canvas. 30 x 23 1/2
London, Tate Gallery

The painting has a moral purpose: Hunt wanted to depict the rebirth of conscience in a "fallen woman." She starts up, staring, as if summoned by a divine voice, abandoning her protector's lap. Every detail has a meaning: the crumpled glove thrown down on the rug signifies the fate that awaits a kept woman, who risks being abandoned to degradation and despair; the ribbons on the ground symbolize the ties that enchain the lost soul; the clock shows Virtue taking Love prisoner; and the engraving behind it is entitled "The Misunderstanding." Of all of these emblems (and many others), the most remarkable is the cat crouched under the table. In contrast to the lover, who as yet understands nothing, the cat has perceived the woman's intention. It releases its prey, a bird, which flees, leaving several feathers under the cat's claws. The parallel is clear: like the bird, the soul touched by Grace will regain its freedom and lift itself up towards God. Here, for once, the cat is cast, though rather involuntarily, in a noble role.   E.F.-W.

184

ÉDOUARD MANET

Paris, 1832 — 1883

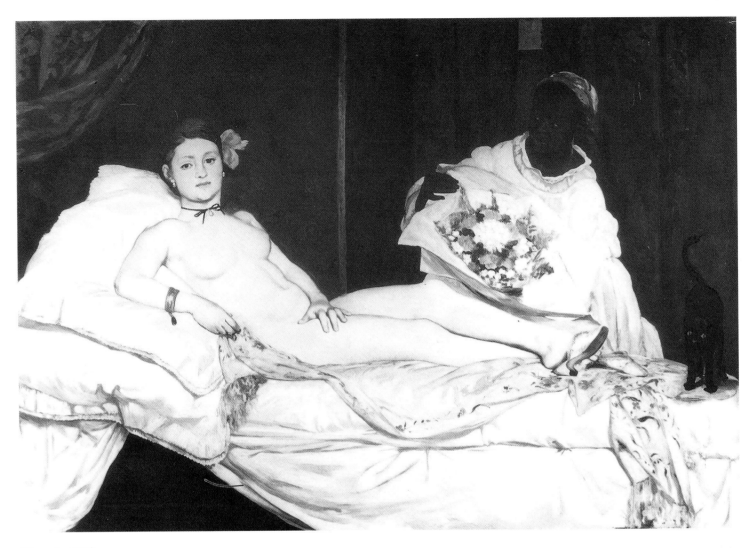

Olympia, 1863
Canvas. 51 1/4 x 74 3/4
Paris, Musée d'Orsay

Of all the cats in Western painting, surely the cat in the *Olympia* has inspired the greatest flood of ink. In our epoch the poor animal has inevitably been the target of the most muddled Freudian-erotic commentary. Let us refrain from adding to all this and state only that the painter's contemporaries saw the cat as a purely painterly motif, not as a "message" with four feet. Zola, for example, observed merely: "you needed some black spots, and in one corner you placed a Negress and a cat." We may add that when Manet painted Zola's portrait some five years later, Zola posed before a reproduction of *Olympia,* but the right side of it was cut off by the portrait, and thus the cat is missing. The cat is actually almost indistinguishable from the dark green curtain in the background. Nevertheless it did not escape the notice of artists who have amused themselves by caricaturing the picture. In 1970, the American artist Larry Rivers exhibited two superimposed *Olympia*s: one of the ladies was black, and had a white servant and a snowy, immaculate cat (Paris, Musée National d'Art moderne). Manet himself played off the black-white opposition several years later, this time in a feline milieu: his poster *Le Rendez-vous des Chats*, created in 1868 for the publication of his friend Champfleury's book *Les Chats,* shows two cats amid the rooftops of Paris. One is white, the other, black. The latter, with its question-mark tail, seems to have come straight from the padded, silken prison of Olympia's apartment. E.F.-W.

PIERRE-AUGUSTE RENOIR

Limoges, 1841 — Cagnes-sur-Mer, 1919

Young Woman with a Cat
Canvas. 39 x 32 1/4
New York, Private Collection

The many cats in Renoir's works are always associated with women, in adherence to eighteenth-century tradition. The most famous of these animals is undoubtedly the one that nestles in the lap of a young woman, sleeping lasciviously, in a picture at the Clark Institute in Williamstown.

"Renoir can do anything—anything he wants to do. Have you seen his cat playing with a ball of multicolored yarns?" wrote Ambroise Vollard. And according to Arsène Alexandre, Degas exclaimed before one of Renoir's paintings: "One would think a cat had painted it!" Was he alluding to the "scratched on" effect of the painter's brushwork, or was he rather referring to the artist's suppleness of treatment, the model's voluptuousness?

Viewed from behind, this cat places its paws on the rim of a flower pot and seems to want to sniff the shrub's pink and white flowers.

P.R.

CECILIA BEAUX

Philadelphia, 1863 — New York, 1942

Sita and Sarita, 1896
Canvas. 37 x 24 3/4
Paris, Musée d'Orsay

Cecilia Beaux's mother, Mrs. Walter Turle, born Sarah A. Lewitt and nicknamed Sarita, shares this portrait with her cat Sita. The artist was so pleased with the canvas that she executed another version many years later (Washington, D.C., Corcoran Gallery of Art). By introducing this affectionate black cat, Beaux transformed an ordinary portrait into an endearing work tinged with mystery. We see no more of the cat than its splendid golden eyes, which stare at us from the same level as the model's grey-green eyes. The latter, garbed all in white, seems lost in thought as her cat examines us. Is Sita's presence inspired by that of its fellow in *Olympia* (see pp. 186–87)? The matter is open to speculation.   P.R.

ANDREW L. VON WITTKAMP

American, nineteenth century

Black Cat Lying on a Chair, 1850–1860
Canvas. 35 3/4 x 29 1/4
Boston, Museum of Fine Arts,
Karolik Collection

Nothing is known of Von Wittkamp, the artist who signed this picture. He is assumed to have been American. The composition of the work is willfully audacious. A black cat sprawls along a chair of simple design; its silhouette stands out sharply against the somber wall. Only the white of the cup of milk and the molding illuminate the composition. The taste for minute details rendered in *trompe-l'oeil* (the knots of the flooring, the fly on the rim of the saucer), the attempt to construct the space through the use of clearly marked diagonals, and the rather naive indication of the shadows cast by the chair and by the cat's tail, all betray an amateur at work. The black cat, the scene's protagonist, amuses more than it intrigues or disturbs.   P.R.

PAUL RANSON

Limoges, 1864 — Paris, 1909

The Sorceress and the Cat, 1893
Canvas. 35 1/2 x 28 1/4
Private Collection

L ike the artist's wife, whom Maurice Denis depicted during the same period drinking tea in the company of a tabby (Saint-Germaine-en-Laye, Musée du Prieuré), Ranson loved cats. He therefore eschewed a traditional representation of the cat as a maleficent inhabitant of scenes of sorcery such as Alessandro Magnasco produced in the eighteenth century. The black cat (silhouetted against a red background, the obligatory sabbath hue) stretches a paw gently toward a black bird that seems much more frightening, as does the horned black monster to the right. The sorceress, sunk in thought, is indifferent to this exotic menagerie.

Ranson wished above all to create a decorative work, red and black, in which flat forms stood out against curving lines—nothing unusual in the decorative system of Art Nouveau. He slipped various hardly distinguishable, esoteric symbols into the composition, such as the astrological sign of Mercury (a circle and cross) that hovers over the sorceress's head. In the star, which contains an inverted crescent, some tangled Hebrew characters can be dimly discerned.

But it is the admirably stylized cat with its arched tail that occupies the place of honor. E.F.-W.

ÉDOUARD VUILLARD

Cuiseaux, 1868 — La Baule, 1940

Portrait of Théodore Duret, 1912
Oil on board. 37 1/2 x 29 1/2
Washington, D.C., National Gallery
of Art, Chester Dale Collection

Théodore Duret (1838–1927) was the subject of many portraits. The republican journalist—a friend of Zola, an art critic and defender of Courbet and Manet, a collector of Degas, Cézanne, Monet and all of the avant-garde painters of his day (his sale in 1894 created a sensation)—posed for Whistler (New York, Metropolitan Museum), and Manet (Paris, Petit Palais), as well as Vuillard. Here the Nabi master shows Duret surrounded by his books and the paintings in his new collection (Whistler's portrait of him, a Tiepolo, a drawing by Van Gogh), holding his cat Lulu in his lap.

Lulu plays more than a minor role in the composition. There is evidence that the cat was the writer-collector's only companion. The world of the cat and the world of Duret harmoniously intertwine. With candor and finesse, Vuillard has captured the perfect rapport that exists between the aged critic and his small comrade.   P.R.

PIERRE BONNARD

Fontenay-aux-Roses, 1867 — Le Cannet, 1947

The White Cat, 1894
Oil on board. 20 x 13
Paris, Musée d'Orsay

Like Bonnard's other cats—he owned many and often painted them—*The White Cat* is nameless, while we know the names of all the painter's dogs: Black, a spaniel; Ubu and Poucette, basset hounds; not to mention Bella and Ravageau, which belonged to Bonnard's younger sister (according to Bonnard's grand-nephew Antoine Terrasse).

Bonnard was attracted by the natural suppleness of the cat's body, which furnished a point of departure for his artistic voyaging. Here Bonnard's cat arches its back more than is physically possible, as if the artist wanted to exaggerate this characteristic feline pose to the point of deformity, almost caricature. The preliminary sketches for the picture are revealing. Drawn from life, they are faithful to reality; in the finished work itself, however, *japonisme* prevails. The animal's head sinks into its body, its eyes become long slits, its legs are stretched, and its tail forms a perfect capital *S*. E.F.-W.

193

BRUNO LILJEFORS

Uppsala, 1860 — Stockholm, 1939

Jeppe in a Flowering Meadow, 1884
Canvas. 48 1/2 x 25 1/2
Private Collection

I t was often said that Liljefors could hear the grass growing, such was his love of nature. Here we can almost hear this cat gliding through the dandelions and flowering clover. The animal is none other than the painter's own Jeppe, with whom Liljefors struck up an acquaintance in Quarnbo, near Uppsala, in the summer of 1884. He carried Jeppe off with him at the end of his sojourn. As a painter Liljefors greatly admired the nuances of Jeppe's gray tabby coat and the black pads of the cat's paw, which he compared to coffee beans.

Momentarily abandoning his accustomed subjects—wild animals or Scandinavian shore birds—Liljefors depicts his new friend as a bit lonesome and apprehensive in this vast stretch of grass and flowers, where it proceeds with infinite caution—an attitude the artist has captured true to life, as cats are indeed often ill at ease when they venture out into the open.

E.F.-W.

JOHN SLOAN

Lock Haven, Pennsylvania, 1871 — Hanover, New Hampshire, 1951

Back Yard in Greenwich Village, 1914
Canvas. 10 1/4 x 12 1/2
New York, Whitney Museum of
American Art

I n a desolate little courtyard, two children build a snowman. Meanwhile, from a window on the far right, a little girl gleefully watches two cats. The first advances cautiously over the roof as its comrade huddles for warmth.

An important painter of the Ashcan School, Sloan dedicated himself to depicting street scenes and everyday life in New York's poorer sections.

The two cats alone cannot brighten up the sad winter day in this bleak courtyard. Their black pelts and gray shadows are etched against the snow. Their vitality, poses, and pastimes are captured with surety. Possessed of no symbolic significance, they are part and parcel of the scene in this disadvantaged neighborhood.   P.R.

GEORGES ANTOINE ROCHEGROSSE

Versailles, 1859 — El Biar, Algeria, 1938

Rochegrosse, who painted an Eastern world that was at once imaginary and conventional, could not resist including in his Egyptian scenes the animal that, to Western eyes, best symbolized and summed up Egypt and its religion. Here is a quartet of felines who, in truth, seem no more vowed to a divine destiny than their four-footed brethren elsewhere. In the background two cats, one black-and-white, one all black, crouch to feed at the feet of a marabou stork, which seems unconcerned by their presence; a third cat, also black and doubtless sated, walks with its tail in the air toward the couple in the center, rejoining another black cat that the young princess strokes in her lap. Like the extremely studied furniture, the costumes and various objects placed here and there, the cats are there to lend local color to this genre scene. Rochegrosse, who wished to be "truer than history," used this narrative approach in his attempts at historical reconstruction, which prefigured, in a sense, the cinematic era's later efforts along the same lines.   E.F.-W.

196

In the Age of the Pharaohs, 1887
Canvas. 22 3/4 x 29 1/4 Ghent, Musée des Beaux-Arts

PAUL GAUGUIN

Paris, 1848 — Atuana, Marquesas Islands, 1903

Where Did We Come From? What Are We?
Where Are We Going?, 1897
Canvas. 54 3/4 x 147 1/4
Boston, Museum of Fine Arts

The fact that Gauguin placed a pair of cats right in the center of his masterpiece must intrigue those who attach more importance to the artist's conscious or unconscious intentions than they do to the work itself.

It is known that Gauguin himself said that the left of the picture alludes to humanity's past, and the right to its future, and that the man in the middle ponders the meaning of existence and stretches his arms towards the fruit of the Tree of Knowledge.

Are the two young cats—one dozing, paws folded beneath itself, the other thrusting its paws straight out in front—purely ornamental, or did Gauguin intend them to mean something more? Do they symbolize innocence, as does the little boy with his back to them?

Whatever the case, one admires their white fur, spotted with gray and green; and one cannot miss the obvious sympathy with which Gauguin treats them.

P.R.

198

PAUL SIGNAC

Paris, 1863 — 1935

Parisian Sunday, 1888–1890
Canvas. 59 x 59
Paris, Private Collection

In this work Signac has admirably described "*l'ennui bourgeois*, amid a decor of potted plants and Henri II chairs . . . In the image of the woman who, as her husband pokes the fire, turns her back on him to gaze out the window at a better day in which one can flee away, there is a tang of suburban Bovary that is not without poetry" (Francoise Cachin, *Paul Signac,* 1971).

The painting's title might easily be "Every man for himself." Even the cat seems uninterested in the domestic circle. Signac paints it in silhouette so that it stands out against the waxed floor. Tail aloft, paws delicately poised on the rug, it, too, looks out the window.   P.R.

MAURICE DENIS

Granville, 1870 — Saint-Germain-en-Laye, 1943

Portrait of the Kapferer Children,
or *The Snack,* 1919
Canvas. 51 1/4 x 35 1/2
Geneva, Petit Palais

This armchair, doubtless unknown to furniture connoisseurs, is singular indeed. Its high back is adorned with the silhouette of a creeping cat whose sinuous grace is worthy of an Art Nouveau wood sculpture. The image in question is in fact a live feline, engaged in a perilous balancing act. Cats are frequently present (although not as audaciously as this one) in Denis's works, for instance, the completely unexpected little tabby at the foot of the easel in the painter's serious *Hommage à Cézanne* (Paris, Musée d'Orsay). Some of the cats in drawings or paintings (Musée du Prieuré in Saint-Germain-en-Laye and various private collections) have been identified, such as the tabby Pilou, the black Symbolo, and Gomonénou, a large striped Breton cat who was christened in honor of the harbor buoy at the mouth of the port of Perros-Guirec, where, according to the artist's daughter Dominique Denis, the painter and his family spent their vacations at the famous villa "Silencio."   E.F.-W.

ANDRÉ DERAIN

Chatou, 1910 — Garches, 1954

The Painter and His Family, ca. 1939
Canvas. 69 1/4 x 48 1/2
London, Tate Gallery

Paintbrush in hand, Derain is depicted at home in Chambourcy, surrounded by family members. His wife Alice reads in the foreground; her niece Geneviève stands behind Derain; and in the background his sister-in-law Suzanne enters, carrying a tray. Even the animals have names: the dog is Finette and the cat is Pitou. Only the two birds are anonymous.

In this ambitious, monumental, and exceedingly strange composition, the parrot and peacock play a decorative role, but their inescapable, white-ringed stares contribute also to the group's unique character. No less disturbing, the curiously active cat Pitou is the only other creature that looks straight into our eyes. All the others seem immobile, absent, plunged into an enigmatic silence of great poetic intensity.

E.F.-W.

GUSTAVE DE SMET

Ghent, 1877 — Deurle, 1943

The Family, 1933
Canvas. 52 x 45 1/2
Brussels, Musées royaux
des Beaux-Arts de Belgique

The cat is a member of the family. "He too has obligingly assumed the pose," according to M.-J. Chartrain-Hebbelinck's astute analysis, "visibly conscious of being an integral part of this human group." De Smet has depicted the cat as robustly as he did the other family members, who are shown frontally (as was common during this period) with massive, large-shouldered forms, their faces rather naively stylized. Like the little girl, the cat stares straight into our eyes, whereas the man and woman divert their gazes slightly, introducing an element of diversity and distinguishing their grown-up world from that of childhood, to which the cat, probably the little girl's playmate, belongs. In fact, the cat and girl exist outside of time in comparison to the responsible parents who have taken time off to pose for the painter. Not merely an anecdotal detail, the cat contributes to the somber sternness of this monumental portrait done in shades of ocher and brown, which established De Smet as one of the finest representatives of Flemish Expressionism in a rather temperate period, the thirties.   E.F.-W.

MARIUS BORGEAUD

Pully, Switzerland, 1861 — Paris, 1924

Interior with Two Glasses, 1923
Canvas. 38 1/4 x 51 1/4
Lausanne,
Musée cantonal des Beaux-Arts

The Swiss painter Marius Borgeaud has not been given the recognition he deserves by twentieth-century art historians, as this work makes clear.

The viewer's eye is riveted by the table covered with a red tablecloth, upon which are two empty glasses, an envelope, and a bouquet of dahlias. Two chairs, an open door, a window that looks out onto a sea or lake, a coffee mill and coffeepot furnish the sunlit room. A black hat is the only indication of man's presence. The cat—also deep black—looks out the window. Its function, amid the play of red, ocher, brown and black, and the skillful rhythm of the straight and curved lines, is not inconsiderable. It relieves the composition's schematicism and infuses the scene with life.   P.R.

SUZANNE VALADON

Bessines-sur-Gartempe, Haute-Vienne, 1867 — Paris, 1938

*Portrait of Miss Lily Walton
with Raminou*, 1922
Canvas. 39 1/4 x 31 3/4
Paris, Musée national d'Art moderne,
Centre Georges-Pompidou

M iss Walton, who was then governess for the Valadon-Utter-Utrillo family, sits in the studio on the rue Cortot in Paris. On her lap reposes a not-inconsequential member of the family of artists—Raminou, both an exemplary model and one of the most celebrated cats in modern painting. Valadon "portrayed" Raminou in many poses: in 1920, held in Lison's arms; in the same year, in two different pictures, all alone on a cloth; and in 1932, lying on a round iron table. The huge cat with its deep gold eyes and ruddy tabby coat perfectly matches the warm colors to which its mistress was so partial. Here it also harmonizes with Miss Walton's flaming tresses. Faced with their convergent gazes, we almost forget that one comes from a handsome house cat and the other from a governess, so equal is the footing upon which they have been placed.   E.F.-W.

FRANZ MARC

Munich, 1880 — Verdun, 1916

Four Cats at Play, 1913
Canvas. 17 1/4 x 26
Stuttgart, Staatsgalerie

To "animalize" art, to create a kind of pantheistic fusion between nature and animals, was Marc's aim in his paintings. For him, animals more closely approached the ideals of Beauty and Purity than Man. He painted horses and above all roe deer, but he also often drew and painted cats between 1908 and 1913. The artist himself chose the title *Vier spielende Katzen*—four cats at play. Marc was careful to give his pictures titles that would assist viewers in deciphering their content, which is not always immediately apparent.

The cats' very geometric bodies, emphasized by broken lines, overlap with one another along intersecting diagonal lines that impart a marvelous sense of motion. The supple arabesques formed by the cats' tails are the only curves. Two cats are white, one is gray, and one green; thus, like the deer that melts into the fir trees of the great German forest, the cats melt into their environment and adopt its color. The cats' forms are still visible, but we sense already the birth of abstraction. In contrast with Van der Leck, who at the same point in his evolution toward abstraction painted a completely immobile cat, Marc disembodies, almost dissolves the cats' forms through the creation of motion. In doing so he engages in a fusion of the experiments of the Futurists and of Robert Delaunay, whose works had struck him so forcefully on his trip to Paris several months earlier.   E.F.-W.

FERNAND LÉGER

Argentan, 1881 — Gif-sur-Yvette, 1955

Woman with a Cat, 1921
Canvas. 36 1/4 x 25 1/2
Hamburg, Kunsthalle

Cats and books have been associated ever since the latter were invented. It is fascinating to see Léger, a painter who cleaves to modernity above all, put his personal stamp on their union in this painting and in a larger version that was formerly housed in the Reber collection in Lausanne.

A black cat, ears pricked, is seated on its mistress's lap. Its black silhouette balances the young woman's mass of black hair. It is surprising to see a cat occupying such a place in a post-Cubist masterpiece. Léger has succeeded perfectly in his small but quite intentional bit of provocation.

                                                                        P.R.

207

BART VAN DER LECK

Utrecht, 1876 — Blaricum, 1958

The Cat, 1914
Casein on fibrocement. 14 1/2 x 11 1/2
Otterlo, Rijksmuseum Kröller-Müller

This quasi-geometric representation of a cat (even down to its muzzle, at the center of the picture), in which all indication of volume or movement is forsaken, is a challenge, considering felines' supple and undulant mobility. A similar tendancy toward stylization was found, according to the artist, in the Egyptian art that he had "discovered" some years earlier in the Louvre, and he applied this treatment also to this model and to the hunters, firemen, and masons who people his other works from the same period. But unlike Van der Leck's humans, who are painted with their bodies looking straight on and faces in profile, the cat is shown with its body in profile and its head toward us, as if Van der Leck were loth to forgo depicting a cat's most fascinating characteristic: its gaze. An amusing and significant note is that in Van der Leck's works dogs, which many consider to be more "human" than cats, are always shown entirely in profile. The cat's vivid glower contrasts with the animal's sharply geometrical body, which bears no suggestion of fur and etches itself in a linear way against the neutral white background, without substance, without weight, abstract already. This completely hieratic—not to say hieroglyphic—cat (how different it is from Franz Marc's "dynamic" cats, see p. 206), so captivated Helene Kröller-Müller, the wife of the great Dutch collector and Maecenas, that she purchased it on sight, during the same period in which Van der Leck began his great decorative work for the Müller firm.   E.F.-W.

FÉLIX VALLOTTON

Lausanne, 1865 — Paris, 1925

Two Cats Passing By
Canvas. 26 x 21 1/2
Switzerland, Private Collection

M ore than Chagall or Balthus, more even than Bonnard, and much more than his Swiss compatriot Steinlen, Vallotton (whose admirable painting of a white cat, *Idleness,* dates from 1896) is one of the great cat-painters of our century.

In a heat-hammered village street—probably in Cannes—two cats unhurriedly make their way in Indian file. The orange-and-white tom (or is it a female?) and the black cat with a white belly are the heroes of the painting, the lords of the village.

Vallotton has marvelously captured the sharp, deep shadows of summer, the desertion of the village—it is the hour of *siesta*—and the familiar, reassuring cats, who are quite at home on this badly paved street. P.R.

GEORG SCHRIMPF

Lockhausen, near Munich, 1889 — Berlin, 1938

Still Life with Cat, 1923
Canvas. 23 1/2 x 17 3/4
Munich, Bayerische
Staatsgemäldesammlungen

This peaceful still life, which centers on such a small, sweet kitten, has nothing to do with the aggressive realism that generally characterizes the *Neue Sachlichkeit* ("New Objectivity") of which Schrimpf was an adherent. This often cruel and provocative style arose in Germany between the two World Wars as a reaction against Expressionism. Here the humbleness of the subject—a simple kitchen, with washing utensils and linen hanging to dry—is tempered, even transfigured, by the artist's treatment of the objects as volumes rather than as utilitarian items: their exaggeratedly smooth surfaces lend them an utterly Classical monumentality. By virtue of its thick, velvety fur, the gray-striped cat, smaller even than the pitcher in the foreground, contrasts with the almost incorporeal coldness of the assembled objects. Motionless, attentive, looking like a small plush toy that one would like to stroke, it irresistibly attracts our eyes. In fact, it is the only element to escape the implacable stoniness with which Schrimpf imbued his still lifes and figurative works, after his trip to Italy in 1922.

E.F.-W.

KEES VAN DONGEN

Delfshaven, near Rotterdam, 1877 — Monte Carlo, 1968

Reading, 1911
Canvas. 57 x 57
Paris, Private Collection

Aaccording to the painter's daughter Dolly, this work was executed in 1911 at 6 rue Saulnier, Van Dongen's Paris studio. The young lady reading a work by Rabelais is the artist's wife Gus Van Dongen (born Augusta Preitinger), whom the artist married in 1901. The cat has remained anonymous, unlike the cats painted by Van Dongen's contemporaries such as André Derain and Suzanne Valadon. This picture, more linear and stylized than most of Van Dongen's works (one notes the play of the stripes on Gus's bodice and on the tablecloth, and the cut-out treatment of the sails in the picture hanging on the wall) rivals a Matisse in its schematicism. Clearly intended as a decorative work, it adorned the hall of 29 Villa Saïd in Paris, the house in which Van Dongen lived from 1915 to 1921, and hung next to a Buddha and above a Far Eastern vase used to hold canes and umbrellas. The little cat is streamlined, smooth, and tailless—at first glance, one mistakes the fold of the bedspread upon which it lies for its tail. Its half-closed eye is the same almond shape as its mistress's "Egyptian" eye—and the eyes of most of the women Van Dongen painted—but lacks her dusky pupil. Van Dongen, who captured Woman's gaze, here depicts Cat's non-gaze.   E.F.-W.

211

HENRI ROUSSEAU

Laval, 1844 — Paris, 1910

Portrait originally identified as Pierre Loti;
probably Edmond Achille Frank,
before 1906
Canvas. 24 x 19 1/2
Zürich, Kunsthaus

Pierre Loti or Edmond Achille Frank? The painting was long considered a portrait of Loti (1850–1923). The evidence seemed convincing: the model bore an undeniable resemblance to the naval officer-writer, who had a taste for both exotic clothes (indicated by the fez) and for cats—Loti had visiting cards made up for his pets ("Madame Moumoutte, white, the foremost cat of Monsieur Pierre Loti, 141, rue Chanzy, Rochefort-sur-Mer"). But in 1952 a certain Edmond Achille Frank, a writer by trade, claimed to be the man in the picture. The proofs he brought to bear, which Francois Le Targat, after Henri Certigny, completely summed up, are difficult to discredit (nevertheless, Rousseau specialists hesitate to accept them). Frank declared, moreover, that he had destroyed his portrait, and that the painting in Zurich is actually only a replica that Rousseau painted for the "museum of horrors" owned by Courteline, the work's first known proprietor.

There remains the large striped cat "to my right, its chest streaked with rectilinear stripes" (Frank, 1952). Although Rousseau forgot its whiskers (though not those of his human model), he admirably captured its profound gaze and, above all, its hieratic presence. Rousseau—a naive painter? P.R.

212

HENRI MATISSE

Le Cateau-Cambrésis, 1869 — Nice, 1954

Marguerite with a Black Cat, 1910
Canvas. 33 x 25 1/4
Paris, Private Collection

With the exception of goldfish, animals seldom appear in Matisse's works—although he owned dogs, cats, and "birds by the cageful." Here, however, we see a black cat that has surrendered itself to slumber in the lap of the painter's daughter Marguerite, the future Mme. Georges Duthuit.

Rather than engaging in a study of the cat's psychology and its ties to its young mistress, Matisse has used the animal as an integrating element in this clever, rhythmic work in which lines and colors harmoniously correspond. Indeed, it must be noted that the two greatest painters of our century (see p. 218) have allowed the cat only an auxiliary role in their works. P.R.

JOAN MIRÓ

Barcelona, 1893 — Palma de Majorca, 1983

The Farmer's Wife, 1922–1923
Canvas. 31 3/4 x 25 1/2
Paris, Private Collection

The huge-footed farmer's wife holds a rabbit by its hind paws as its head dangles lamentably. For its part, the cat—a queer beast with black-and-white whiskers unlike any ever seen before—purrs contentedly. According to its custom, it warms itself by the stove, smiling beatifically, or perhaps with ironic sarcasm. Miró's works are not devoid of humor.

P.R.

215

MARC CHAGALL

Vitebsk, 1887 — Paris, 1985

Half Past Three (The Poet), 1911
Canvas. 77 1/4 x 57
Philadelphia, Philadelphia Museum of Art

A cat—a green cat—licks at the poet's coat; the poet's head (green as well) is upside-down; we are deep in the world of Chagall.

Above and beyond any symbolism, any allusion to the foresight of cats (animals possessed of piercing vision), we perceive the Cubist message, which is somewhat "destabilized" by Chagall's approach. The work's lively, unprecedented colors and the cat's pointed tongue and horn-shaped ears indicate that even as Chagall adopts the geometric forms of Cubism he renounces not one iota of his personal vision.

P.R.

PAUL KLEE

Münchenbuchsee, 1879 — Muralto-Locarno, 1940

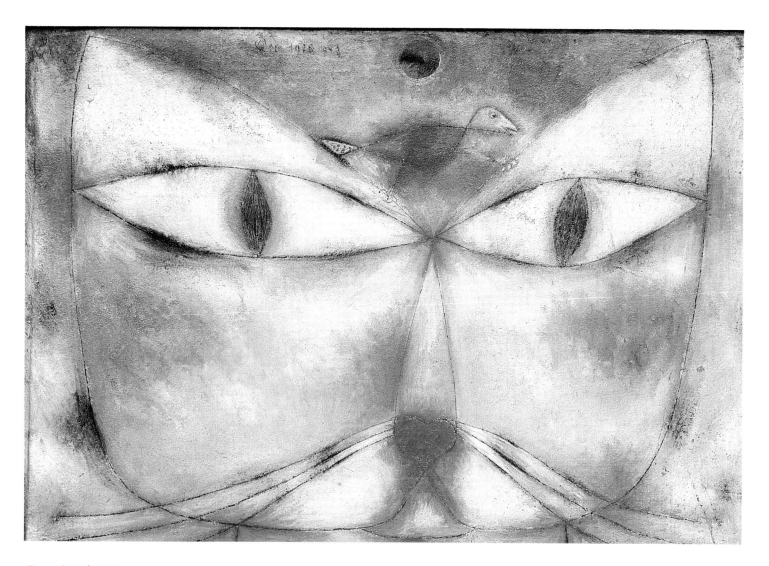

Cat and Bird, 1928
Oil and ink on canvas. 15 x 20 3/4
New York, The Museum of Modern Art

A cat dreams of the bird it longs to devour. The artist has used but one line to draw its head—which occupies the painting's entire space—and its fine whiskers. Its vacant, far-off gaze is focused on its prey. The picture's colors, emerald green and fuschia, accentuate its strangeness and poetry. Oblivious to every-day life, Klee's cat is lost in reverie.   P.R.

PABLO PICASSO

Malaga, 1881 — Mougins, 1973

Cat Devouring a Bird, 1939
Canvas. 31 3/4 x 39 1/4
Paris, Musée Picasso

Picasso, who loved cats, painted relatively few, and these were not always ingratiating (even Jacqueline's black cat, which Picasso often depicted in 1964). Here, the animal holds a vainly fluttering bird in its fangs. Given that it was painted during a doleful period in Picasso's life—the Spanish Civil War—it is not surprising that the cat expresses violence and sadistic pleasure in cruelty.

"The subject obsessed me—I don't know why," said Picasso, who later painted another version of the work (New York, Victor W. Ganz Collection). His depictions of this gray tiger with its long whiskers are unsympathetic portrayals of a harsh reality.   P.R.

BALTHUS

Paris, 1908

The Cat at "La Méditerranée," 1949
Canvas. 50 x 72 3/4
Private Collection

B althus painted cats from his youth (*Mitsou, Forty Images* dates from 1921). His felines are far from innocent: they contribute to the heavy, disturbingly erotic atmosphere favored by the artist. Often they are cats only in appearance and in reality are cruel or deceitful men. The cat at La Méditerranée—a famous seafood restaurant on the Place de l'Odéon in Paris (for which Balthus painted a sign, in adherence with time-honored tradition)—is no exception.

Cats have forever had to steal fish for their repast. But not here. Carried along by a splendid rainbow, the fish fly right onto the plate. The cat—actually a mountebank wearing a grinning cat-mask—prepares to devour them with great relish. P.R.

INDEX OF ARTISTS

PHOTOGRAPHIC CREDITS

P. 45, Ph. Eric Mitchell/ The Philadelphia Museum of Art. P. 46–47, Ph. Scala, Florence. P. 48, Ph. The National Gallery, London. P. 49, Ph. John Webb, London. P. 50–51, Ph. Museum of the Vatican. P. 52, Ph. The Metropolitan Museum of Art, New York. Gift of J. Pierpont Morgan. P. 53, Ph. Joachim Blauel-Artothek, Planneg. P. 54, Ph. Philadelphia Museum of Art. P. 55, Ph. Eric Mitchell/ The Philadelphia Museum of Art. P. 56, Ph. The Ashmolean Museum, Oxford. P. 57, Ph. Bruce C. Jones, New York. P. 60, Ph. Scala, Florence. P. 61, Ph. Alinari-Giraudon, Paris. P. 62–63, Ph. Pedicini, Naples. P. 64–65, Ph. Fototecnica, Vicenze. P. 66–67, Ph. Museum of the Vatican. P. 68, Ph. Musées nationaux, Paris. P. 69, Ph. Hubert Josse, Paris. P. 70–71, Ph. Germanisches National-museum, Nuremberg. P. 72–73, Ph. Jörg Anders/ Staatliche Museen Preussischer Kulturbesistz, Berlin-Ouest. P. 74, Ph. Musées nationaux, Paris. P. 75, Ph. Hubert Josse, Paris. P. 76–77, Ph. Museum Boymans-van Beuningen, Rotterdam. P. 78–79, Ph. Photobusiness, Vienna. P. 80–81, Ph. Photobusiness, Vienna. P. 83, Ph. Hubert Josse, Paris. P. 84–85, Ph. Rijksmuseum, Amsterdam. P. 89, Ph. Finarte. P. 91, Ph. The Metropolitan Museum, New York. P. 94–95, Ph. The Prado, Madrid. P. 96–97, Ph. Royal Palace, Amsterdam. P. 98, Ph. Kunsthistorisches Museum, Vienna. P. 99, Ph. Photobusiness, Vienna. P. 100, Ph. Musées nationaux, Paris. P. 101, Ph. Hubert Josse, Paris. P. 102, Ph. Studio Cardon, Dunkirk. P. 103, Ph. Staatliche Kunstsammlungen, Kassel. P. 105, Ph. Edeltraut/Akademie der bildenden Künste, Vienna. P. 106, Ph. Musées nationaux, Paris. P. 107, Ph. Hubert Josse, Paris. P. 108–109, Ph. Museum voor Schöne Kunsten, Ghent. P. 110–111, Ph. Patrick Delatouche, Orléans. P. 113, Ph. Hubert Josse, Paris. P. 114, Ph. Lucarelli, Nice. P. 115, Ph. Bayerische Staatsammlungen, Munich. P. 116–117, Ph. Alfred Schiller/ Museum of Fine Arts, Budapest. P. 119, Ph. The Cleveland Museum of Art. P. 120, Ph. Offentliche Kunstsammlungen, Basel. P. 121, Ph. Hinz, Basel. P. 122, Ph. Anne Gold/ Suermondt Museum, Aix-La-Chapellé. P. 123, Ph. Staatliche Kunsthalle, Karlsruhe. P. 124–125, Ph. Rijksmuseum, Amsterdam. P. 126–127, Ph. The National Gallery, London. P. 128–129, The Fitzwilliam Museum, Cambridge. P. 130, Ph. Musées nationaux, Paris. P. 132–133, Ph. National Museum, Stockholm. P. 135, Ph. Hubert Josse, Paris. P. 136–137, Ph. The Norton Simon Museum of Art, Pasadena. P. 138, Ph. Agraci, Paris. P. 139, The J. Paul Getty Museum, Malibu, P. 140–141, Ph. The Frick Collection, New York. P. 142, Ph. The National Gallery of Scotland. P. 143, Ph. Mula et Haramati, Tel-Aviv. P. 145. Ph. Musées nationaux, Paris. P. 146, Ph. Giraudon, Paris. P. 147, Ph. Lauros-Giraudon, Paris. P. 149, Ph. Visual studio, Naples. P. 150, Ph. Studio C.N.B., Bologna. P. 151, Ph. Prudence Cuming and Associates, London. P. 152–153, Ph. The Nelson-Atkins Museum of Fine Arts, Kansas City. P. 154, The Prado, Madrid. P. 156, Ph. The Metropolitan Museum of Art, New York. P. 157, Ph. The Metropolitan Museum of Art, New York. P. 158, Ph. The Tate Gallery, London. P. 159, Ph. The Tate Gallery, London. P. 160, Ph. The Metropolitan Museum of Art, New York. P. 161, Ph. The Metropolitan Museum of Art, New York. P. 162, Ph. Musées nationaux, Paris. P. 163, Ph. Hubert Josse, Paris. P. 164, Ph. The Greater London Council, the Iveagh bequest, Kenwood, London. P. 165, Ph. Claude Muzzin, Grasse, P. 167, Ph. Patrice Delatouche, Orléans. P. 168, Ph. Hubert Josse, Paris. P. 170–171, Ph. Ellebé, Rouen, P. 172–173. Ph. Jörg Anders/ Staatliche Museum Preussischer Kulturbesitz, West Berlin. P. 174, Ph. Musée Jean de La Fontaine, Château-Thierry. P. 175, Ph. The Minneapolis Institute of Arts, P. 176–177, Ph. Hutin, Compiégne. P. 178, Ph. Musées nationaux, Paris. P. 179, Ph. Giraudon, Paris. P. 180–181, Ph. The Nelson Atkins Museum of Fine Arts, Kansas City. P. 182–183, Ph. The City Art Galleries, Manchester. P. 184–185, Ph. The Tate Gallery, London. P. 186, Ph. Musées nationaux, Paris. P. 187, Ph. Hubert Josse, Paris. P. 188, Ph. The Metropolitan Museum of Art, New York. P. 189, Ph. Hubert Josse, Paris. P. 190, Ph. The Museum of Fine Arts, Boston. P. 191, Ph. Lemadec, Paris. P. 192, Ph. The National Gallery of Art, Washington. P. 195, Ph. Geoffrey Clements/ The Whitney Museum of Art, New York. P. 196, Ph. Piet Ysabie/ Museum voor Schone Kunsten, Ghent. P. 198–199, Ph. The Museum of Fine Arts, Boston. P. 200, Ph. Agraci, Paris. P. 201, Ph. Musée du Petit Palais, Geneva. P. 203, Ph. Musées royaux des Beaux-Arts de Belgique, Brussels. P. 204, Ph. Musée cantonal des Beaux-Arts, Lausanne. P. 205, Ph. M.N.A.M., Centre Georges-Pompidou, Paris. P. 206, Ph. Staatsgalerie, Stuttgart, P. 207, Ph. Ralph Kleinhempel/ Kunsthalle, Hamburg. P. 208, Ph. Capi-Lux/Rijksmuseum, Kröller-Müller, Otterloo. P. 210, Ph. Joachim Blauel-Artothek. P. 212, Ph. Kunsthaus, Zurich. P. 216, Ph. The Philadelphia Museum of Art. P. 217, Ph. The Museum of Modern Art, New York. P. 218, Ph. Musées nationaux, Paris. P. 219, Ph. Peter Willi, Paris/ Arch. Éditions d'art Albert Skira, Geneva.

ACKNOWLEDGMENTS

We wish to thank all those who have helped us, whether they are cat lovers or not. First of all, we must thank our friends in the Department of Painting at the Louvre, who are too numerous to mention by name. We are especially grateful to those who notified us of several particularly rare or exceptional cats. Then, for all of the various ways in which they lent us assistance, we thank: Henri Baderou, Katharine Baetjer, Yves Beauvalot, Juan de Beistegui, María van Berge-Gerbaud, Maître Blache, Miklos Boskovits, Roland Bossard, Jean-Claude Boyer, Françoise Cachin, Jean-Pierre Camard, Marco Chiarini, Margie Christian, Maurice et Pierre Chuzeville, Philip Conisbee, Anthony Dallas, Henri Defoer, Gemma di Domenico Cortese, Dominique Denis, Jean-Denis Devauges, Claire Dossier, Marie-Anne Dupuy, Raoul Ergmann, Andrea Emiliani, Jean Feray, Bruno Foucart, David Fraser Jenkins, Sydney Freedberg, Marc Fumaroli, Axelle de Gaigneron, Nicole Garnier, Gisela Goldberg, Pontus Grate, E. G. Grimme, Amy Guichard (†), Marguerite Guillaume, Jean Habert, John Hayer, Carlos van Hasselt, Claudette Joannis, Derek Johns, William R. Johnston, Michael Kitson, Balthazar Klossowski de Rola, Geneviève Knupfer, Hans Kraan, Jacques Kuhnmunch, Geneviève Lacambre, Valérie Lavergne, Patrick Le Chanu, Thierry Lefrançois, Pierre Lemoine, Juan José Luna, Patrick Matthiesen, Marc Maurie, Hilaire Metsers, Jennifer Montagu, Josette Meyssard, Philippe Morel, J. W. Niemeijer, G. M. Nock, David Ojalvo, Anna Ottani Cavina, Vicenzo Pacelli, André Pelle, Ann Percy, Bruno Pfàffli, Jean-Michel Pianelli, Edmund P. Pillsbury, Édouard Pommier, Casimiro Porro, Colette Prieur, Wolfgang Prohaska, Juliette Rabbe, Jean Rivière, Anne Roquebert, Gertrude Rosenberg, Robert Rosenblum, Bethsabée de Rothschild, Renato Ruottolo, Jean-Pierre Samoyault, Erich Schleier, Werner Schmidt, C.J.F. van Schooten, David Scrase, Seymour Slive, Nicola Spinosa, Antoine Terrasse, Eric Turquin, Georges Vindry, Henri Wallenberg, Rodolphe et Simone Walter, Leonie von Wilckens, Luce Wilquin, Jayne Wrightsman, Pietro Zampetti, Federico Zeri, Henry V. Zimet. Finally, particular thanks must go to François Bonnefoy, who followed this book through every stage of its preparation.